Reserve Memories

STUDIES IN THE ANTHROPOLOGY
OF NORTH AMERICAN INDIANS

Editors
Raymond J. DeMallie
Douglas R. Parks

RESERVE MEMORIES

The Power of the Past in a Chilcotin Community

David W. Dinwoodie

PUBLISHED BY THE UNIVERSITY OF NEBRASKA PRESS
LINCOLN AND LONDON

IN COOPERATION WITH
THE AMERICAN INDIAN STUDIES RESEARCH INSTITUTE,
INDIANA UNIVERSITY, BLOOMINGTON

Acknowledgment for the use of previously
published material appears on page ix.

Library of Congress Cataloging-in-Publication Data
Dinwoodie, David W., 1961–
Reserve memories : the power of the past in a Chilcotin community / David W.
Dinwoodie.
p. cm. — (Studies in the anthropology of North American Indians)
Includes bibliographical references and index.
ISBN 0-8032-1721-8 (cloth : alk. paper)
ISBN 978-0-8032-2246-5 (paper : alk. paper)
1. Chilcotin Indians—History. 2. Chilcotin Indians—Social life and customs. 3. Chilcotin
mythology—British Columbia—Nemaia Creek valley. 4. Oral tradition—British
Columbia—Nemaia Creek Valley. 5. Nemaia Creek Valley (B.C.)—History. 6. Nemaia
Creek Valley (B.C.)—Social life and customs. I. Title. II. Series.
E99.T78 D56 2002
305.897'2—dc21   2001052239

Dedicated to the memory of
Amelia William
Charlene William
Danny William
Leroy William
William Setah
Noreen Solomon
Scotty Lulua
Timothy Lulua

Contents

List of Illustrations

Map

Tables

Acknowledgments

This book was written with the permission of the Nemiah Valley Indian Band. I am deeply indebted to the Chilcotin people who have made my research possible by sharing aspects of their cultural heritage. I have used pseudonyms in the text with the exception of public figures. I want particularly to thank Henry and Mabel Solomon, Ronnie and Martie Solomon and family, Gilbert Solomon, Bernie and Geraldine Solomon and family, Lennie Solomon and family, Jim and Dinah Lulua and family, Tom and Illa Pierce, Wilfred and Dorinne William, Eugene and Mabel William, Bennie and Celia William, Raphael William, Leona William, Edmund Lulua and June William and family, Roger William and Shannon Stump and family, Ubil and Julianna Lulua, Annie Williams and Walter Lulua and family, Dennis and Suzie Lulua and family, Leslie Stump and Nancy Lulua and family, William Lulua and family, Andrew and Francie Lulua, Lillian Lulua, Madeline Setah, Francis and Agat Setah, David Setah and Margaret Lulua and family, Wayne William and Annie Setah and family, Adam William, Doris William, Norman William, Otis William, Geraldine William, Blaine William, Willard William, Bobby William, Georgina Johnny and Gerry Jack and family, Francis Laceese, Ivor Myers, and Ervin Charleyboy and family. They are not responsible for my mistakes, and these thanks do not mean to suggest that I speak for the Chilcotin people of Nemiah Valley. I am especially grateful for the expertise and patience of my linguistic instructors Gilbert Solomon and Georgina Johnny Sechanalyagh.

I thank Keith H. Basso, Richard Bauman, Robert Brightman, Raymond J. DeMallie, Raymond D. Fogelson, Paul Friedrich, Jason Baird Jackson, Paul D. Kroeber, Robert E. Moore, Suzanne Oakdale, and Michael Silverstein for responding to one or another version of this manuscript.

Part of chapter 1 and most of chapter 4 were previously published in a slightly different form as "Authorizing Voices: Going Public in an Indigenous Language," *Cultural Anthropology* (May 1998), 13(2):193–223. I acknowledge the American Anthropological Association for permission to reprint this material.

I thank the graduate students at the University of New Mexico. Alfred Matiki, Tad McIlwraith, Mariann Skahan, Sarah Soliz, Alan Vince, Erik Wilker, and many others have contributed to the ideas in this book.

I thank my family—my parents David and Marie Dinwoodie, my siblings Ian Dinwoodie and Adrienne Crown, my wife Suzanne Oakdale, and my daughters Emily and Elizabeth—for sustaining my body and soul.

This research was supported by the Melville and Elizabeth Jacobs Fund of the Whatcom Museum, the Phillips Fund of the American Philosophical Society, the Division of Social Sciences at the University of Chicago, the Wenner-Gren Foundation, and the Research Allocations Committee at the University of New Mexico. I am very grateful for the support.

Note on Orthography

In this book I use a modified version of the practical orthography employed by the Chilcotin individuals with whom I worked during my research. This orthography stems from pioneering linguistic work by Michael Krauss, Eung-Do Cook, and several missionary traditions dating back to Fr. Adrien-Gabriel Morice.

The Chilcotin consonantal inventory is, for the purpose of this book, comparable to those of other Athabaskan languages, and the symbols I draw from are widely used in practical orthographies. The Chilcotin vowel inventory, however, is unusual for an Athabaskan language because of historical influences from such surrounding languages as Lillooet (a Salish-family language). The practical orthography in local use represents vowels according to their underlying phonemic values and represents to a significant degree the results of a comparative historical reconstruction of some specific consonant-vowel sequences. I depart from the practical orthography in that I represent vowels phonetically according to their pronunciation within the context of the narratives that are the subject of the book. I follow standard Americanist practice in the representation of these phonetic values.

Reserve Memories

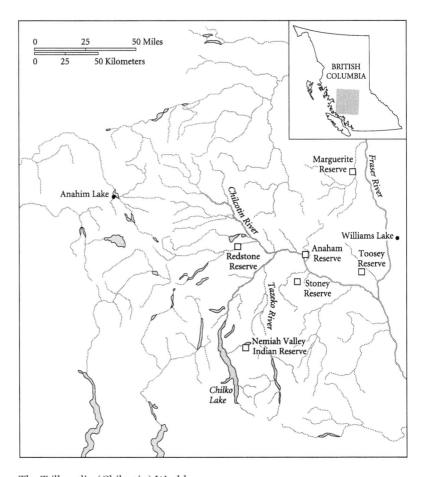

The Tsilhqut'in (Chilcotin) World

Introduction

The present has hitherto been the willing victim of the past; the time has now come when it should turn on the past and exploit it in the interests of advance.

James Harvey Robinson (1912)

At roughly the turn of the last century, the Canadian government essentially forced the Chilcotin people of Nemiah Valley onto Indian reserves in an effort to modernize the state. While Chilcotin people continued their traditions as best they could under the circumstances, they were poorly positioned to effectively maintain their place in the broader world. This study shows that today, at the turn of another century, the Chilcotin people of Nemiah Valley are directly engaging the challenges presented by new neighbors, new generations, and new developments in politics, the economy, and the public sphere. By drawing on their traditional narrative practices as though they represent a kind of cultural reserve, the Chilcotin people of Nemiah Valley are addressing the changing present, fashioning, in essence, modern worlds of their own.

This is a study of historical consciousness among the Chilcotin people of the Nemiah Valley Indian Band of British Columbia, Canada, as they are coming to engage directly the larger social entities in which they live. The study shows that people of the Nemiah Valley Indian Band are neither fashioning a modern history de novo nor borrowing one directly from the West; rather, they are creating history by dynamically applying several varieties of traditional narrative ("myth," "historical narratives") to the circumstances of contemporary reserve life. The more things change, the more they stay the same.

It would not be entirely infelicitous, I believe, to see this as a movement toward a "new" local history, something like "the New History" envisioned by James Harvey Robinson. It is primarily performative rather than representational. It is modern in conception but local in execution. It is partial and pragmatic. Varieties of traditional narrative are not being extended automatically according to a transcendent cultural logic, as structural anthropology once claimed for "cold" societies; nor are they being deployed tactically by autonomous individuals calculating relative advantage in fields of power, as those in the Hobbesian tradition claim for "hot," or modern, societies. Traditional narratives are being creatively extended to contemporary circumstances by persons acting within the rubrics of families, communities, and bands, which is to say, within the rubrics of small, for the most part face-to-face groups engaged in concrete activities. Such middle-range concepts as occasions of speaking, role relations, utterances, narratives, and voices turn out to be more effective tools for analyzing these types of behavior and this kind of movement than social structures, cultural logics, systems of power, or aggregates of freely calculating individuals. The crux of the matter is that people in small groups are orienting themselves in the rapidly shifting present by enlisting memories of efforts to do the same in the past. To give these analogies the quality of operational reality, to paraphrase Stanley Tambiah (1985:53), people are drawing centrally on the voices of ancestors, which is to say, they are drawing on the social alignments evident in the very words the ancestors uttered when addressing and transforming the dynamic worlds in which they once lived.

A Closer View

The application of traditional forms of narrative discourse to new circumstances is particularly salient at Nemiah Valley. Because of geography and historical chance, Nemiah Valley has remained on the economic margins until recently. As a result, the surrounding natural environment is still relatively intact, and band members have been able to continue many of their traditional subsistence activities. Because of the rapidly expanding reach of the Canadian government and economy, band members are increasingly able to participate in public schooling, public health care, government economic programs, the broadcast media, and the local market for labor and goods. The situation at Nemiah Valley, then, is one in which a traditional indigenous community is attempting to maintain its integrity by coming to terms with one of the world's most rapidly developing nation-states. This was brought home to me in a recent experience. In August 1998, on a return visit to the area, I was to interview for the position of coordinator of a Traditional Use Study (TUS) for the Tsilhqut'in National Government. The Department of Forestry of the province of British Columbia initiated the TUS program as part of a new effort to enlist meaningful contributions from Indian bands regarding land use decisions. Forestry would pay bands substantial sums of money to compile hard information on aboriginal use of public lands. The studies were to be conducted on the basis of questionnaires and maps: "Have you ever hunted for moose? If so, indicate the locations of all successful hunts on the government map. Have you ever hunted for bear? If so, . . ." Native bands would receive some protection for the areas of greatest interest to them from the point of view of traditional use, and they would receive substantial financial support (up to millions of dollars) for creating a written record of their history.

Of course, the program is not entirely disinterested. If the overt function is identifying the portions of public land for which Native claims can be substantiated, the covert function is identifying those portions for which Native claims cannot be substantiated. If one goal is assisting Native communities in documenting their ties to the land, the other is expediting extractive leases on Crown (public) lands. In any case, Native leaders are accustomed to evaluating the practical merits of such interested programs. The Tsilhqut'in National Government had already decided by the time of the interview that the program would provide money needed to begin formally documenting Tsilhqut'in culture. The leaders had applied for and won a contract for a TUS, and they were looking for someone to assist in its implementation.

Without knowing exactly what I might be getting into (I had many questions, such as who was in favor of the program, who was participating, whether I would have the full support of the leaders, and so on, not to mention the fact that I was already fully employed at the University of New Mexico), I indicated that I would consider the position. An interview was scheduled for a meeting being held at Nemiah Valley the following week. When I arrived at the Band Office on the day of interview, chiefs and other leaders were conducting the business. At about 11:00 A.M. the host of the meeting, chief of the Nemiah Valley Indian Band, formally invited me into the building's large main room. He was polite but formal. Four long tables were arranged in a square in the center of the room. The chiefs sat along the north side of the tables; the staff of the Tsilhqut'in (Chilcotin) National Government and several other interested people, about sixteen people in all, sat on the other three sides of the square. Elders sat at the margins of the room in small loosely organized clusters. People nodded as I entered the room; again, they were polite but formal.

I was directed to a chair on one corner of the north side of the tables. Each person at the table introduced him- or herself to me in turn. Then they began with the questions. Each in turn read me a question from a printout. How extensive was my training in anthropology? Did I have training in linguistics? Which languages had I studied? Which native languages had I studied? How much did I know about the Chilcotin language? I was asked to list the Chilcotin names of each Chilcotin community, and I was asked about Chilcotin dialects.

People then shifted their attention to questions regarding the nature of the TUS. What did I see as the benefits and liabilities of such a study? Several chiefs wondered whether the study would generate a complete authoritative account of Chilcotin culture. I told them I thought that was unlikely. As I spoke, the expressions on their faces suggested to me that the question had been more for my benefit than for theirs. Someone wondered whether the information might be used for curriculum development, land claims, and cultural preservation. I responded that I thought these were reasonable goals. I was asked whether documenting the culture in this way necessarily involved full disclosure of all community-held information. Would the study necessitate breaching traditional etiquette, or was it possible to conduct the study according to traditional Chilcotin values? How would I decide what information to include and what to exclude? Who would have rights to the material generated in the study? Who would have the copyright on the report? Who would get copyright on information collected but not included in the report? And, for that matter, how did copyright law work in a case like this? As we continued to discuss these questions, I realized that *no one* knew the answers to these questions. These were some of the most vexing questions of our time, no less puzzling and no less intriguing to Internet entrepreneurs, publishers, and civil servants than to these chiefs and sundry leaders sitting in a small Band Office in one of the more remote areas of Canada. Behind the specific inquiries directed at me that day lay two broad questions: How are we to manage our traditions today? Might it not be possible to use our traditions to advance ourselves in the modern world?

As we were talking, I noticed people carrying trays of food and laying them out on a long table. At some point the interview was interrupted for dinner. We arose from our seats and proceeded to the table. In a typically graceful Chilcotin gesture, people made way for me to eat first. Gazing at the table I saw salmon (the salmon were running at the time), turkey, potatoes, freshly made bannock, and so many other dishes that I cannot remember them all now. The conversations shifted to food, weather, and the renewal of old acquaintances as we loaded our plates with steaming food. We dispersed in small groups to eat, and conversations bubbled along like so many percolating coffee pots. As I ate and talked quietly with old friends, it slowly became apparent to me that the meal was not being treated as a mere lunch; it was a feed. In appreciation for their traditional ties to the many communities represented by the various leaders, local band members of Nemiah Valley had prepared a feast for the meeting. In other words, the structure of the event—the embedding of unfolding issues within received ways of doing things—recapitulated in certain respects the subject matter of the meeting, just as the subject matter for the meeting recapitulated themes built into the structure of traditional collective gatherings. Seeing the embedding of tradition in contemporary life, and the fact that a space for change had long been present in traditional practice, seemed to temper the shock of encountering difficult and cutting-edge questions about intellectual property rights in one of the more remote parts of North America. As I sipped a cup of coffee relaxing after a second or third helping, trying to come to terms with all of this, someone tapped on a microphone, and we returned to the business at hand.

The meeting shows the Chilcotin leadership focusing full attention on relations between past and present in the context of the changing political economic environment of contemporary reserve life. It also shows that the community at Nemiah Valley saw this as a traditional activity. What the meeting does not show is that in family homes and gatherings, regular Chilcotin people too find themselves questioning the terms of the present and responding by activating select traditional practices, in particular, traditional narrative genres. The aim of this book is to document this narrative historicization of the present as best as possible from the vantage of contemporary linguistic and cultural anthropology.

The Dynamics of Historical Narrative

The most logical framework for studying the situated use of narrative, whether historical or not, is the ethnography of speaking, or the ethnography of communication. While the lines of thought in this approach are so diverse that they defy encapsulation, the most visible emphases in the ethnography of speaking have been (1) elucidating the correlations between speech genres and social settings by reference to local taxonomies (Gossen 1974; Sherzer 1983) and (2) examining performance as a factor in shaping verbal traditions. The most encompassing work in the taxonomy of speech genre vein is Gary Gossen's *Chamulas in the World of the Sun* (1974). Gossen details a five-level taxonomy embracing virtually every variety of speech used in the community. Gossen's analysis, observe Charles Briggs and Richard Bauman, "underscores the productiveness of a systemic ethnographic perspective as against a focus on selected or privileged genres (e.g., myth) alone, or on mere generic inventories" (1992:139).

Approaches to performance within the ethnography of speaking have attempted to account for the fact that the circumstances in which they are performed determine how some "texts" are realized. Research in this area has shown that the resulting variation is not incidental to verbal traditions but, rather, generative of them (Bauman 1986; Duranti 1984; Hymes 1981; Sherzer 1983:118–120).

These two complementary approaches unquestionably provide a foundation for the study of the sociocultural significance of linguistic practice. Yet they share a common assumption that ultimately limits their utility, that being the assumption that communicative systems are functionally integrated with the social order constituted in material terms. This assumption is evident in the goal of the ethnography of speaking—"to elucidate [ethnographically] the patterns and functions of speaking as a cultural system or as part of cultural systems organized in other terms" (Bauman and Sherzer 1989:xi)—and is in its unifying principle—"that society and culture are communicatively constituted, and that no sphere of social or cultural life is fully comprehensible apart from speaking as an instrument of its constitution" (Bauman and Sherzer 1989:xi).

My experience at Nemiah Valley shows that we cannot assume that there is synchronic functional integration of communicative and material aspects of society. For example, the most prominent buildings in the valley are the school and the Band Office. Both buildings are relatively new and relatively large: one is made of brick, the other, stonework. Other structures include a log church of notably modest proportions, frame or log houses discretely dispersed throughout the woods, wooden slat smokehouses, and the occasional crumbling root cellar. For some time I tried to determine whether the relative size of architectural structures might not serve as a guide to what sorts of ideas people apply to daily events. I could only establish that one would be gravely mistaken to infer from the prominence of the school and the Band Office, or from the budgets of either institution, that life at Nemiah these days is shaped foremost by Western enlightenment thinking and centralized, liberal politics.

In more specific terms the problem is that the more one becomes attuned to the situation, the more one recognizes that Chilcotin varieties of historical narrative are not always functionally integrated with the dominant institutional orders of the time as these present themselves to the senses. Like certain varieties of talk occurring in the interstices, they happen expressly "not to be geared *into* [the] extensive social projects" of the present (Goffman 1974:501). They are in neither a functional nor a dysfunctional relationship with the workings of tribal/national government, the church, or cultural revival as these are being conducted in the schools. They cannot be understood, in fact, in terms of a monolithic conceptualization of function. They represent neither public acquiescence nor hidden transcripts (Scott 1990).

This lack of synchronic functional integration poses serious problems for the ethnography of communication as it has been conceptualized, as noted in a recent critical review of anthropological uses of the concept of genre. Charles Briggs and Richard Bauman observe that "the broadest contrast that characterizes understandings of genre in linguistic anthropology (and, we might add, in adjacent disciplines) sets off those approaches that constitute genre as an orderly and ordering principle in the organization of language,

society, and culture from those that contend with the elements of disjunction, ambiguity, and general lack of fit that lurk around the margins of
generic categories, systems, and texts" (1992:144–145). They argue that the
approaches that view genre exclusively as an "orderly and ordering principle" are poorly suited to addressing the ethnographic realities of the present,
and this certainly is in accord with the situation at Nemiah Valley. The
acknowledgment of the limitations of assuming functional integration represented in this work marks a step forward in the ethnography of communication to be sure. Nevertheless, what seems remarkable at Nemiah Valley is
not simply the presence of "disjunction, ambiguity, and general lack of fit"
but also people's capacity for surmounting these. If synchronic functional
integration would not make a productive assumption in this case, neither
would its polar opposite.

To approach the "present" as it is understood locally at Nemiah Valley,
one must become attuned to ideas that were generated in the past. It is not so
much that ideas have no basis in material reality but, rather, that the material
reality that counts is not necessarily the one directly available to the senses.
In other words, there is a sort of discrepancy between material reality and
conceptual reality as these are given in any particular moment, between
the planes of "things-as-they-appear-to-objective-observers" and "things-
as-they-are-to-locals," between, in a sense, the immediacy of the past and
the overabundance of the present. The Chilcotin people of Nemiah Valley
bridge this gap as a matter of course in the practice of their traditional
culture according to the exigencies of the present. That they do so is not
an insignificant fact—it just happens to be one to which they have become
accustomed.

This discrepancy, in my opinion, is a function of the rapidity of social
change in the greater environment in which the community of Nemiah
Valley is embedded and the challenge this presents for a small community
trying to encompass the present within a coherent frame. If, from their
point of view, they are doing no more than continuing their ways, it is
remarkable that they can do so in what in an anthropological perspective
seems to be a time of extremely rapid global change.

Assuming, then, that the gap between appearances and conceptual realities is essentially determined by the relative paces of two social orders, we
might well consider the possibility that the anthropology of history, which
concerns itself with such matters as historicities, might provide some guid-
ance for developing an approach to the ethnography of speaking more
suited to the challenges faced by the ethnographer of contemporary Native North American society. Marshall Sahlins's goal in recent work is to

develop a theoretically coherent way of addressing historical change from the point of view of local communities. He has focused on situations that from the vantage of European historians and other outsiders have been seen as indicative of ruptures in traditional practice but which from the vantage of local participants are understood as extensions of traditional practice. Sahlins makes the gap between outward appearances and local realities the central analytical focus for his approach by distinguishing among "structure," "event," and "the structure of the conjuncture." A "structure," for Sahlins, is a symbolic scheme very much in accord with Lévi-Strauss's sense of the term. An event, Sahlins observes, "is not simply a phenomenal happening, even though as a phenomenon it has reasons and forces of its own, apart from any given symbolic scheme. An event becomes such as it is interpreted. Only as it is appropriated in and through the cultural scheme does it acquire an historical *significance*" (1985:xiv). An event is thus not to be diametrically opposed to a structure. Rather, it represents "a relation between a happening and a structure (or structures): an encompassment of the phenomenon-in-itself as a meaningful value, from which follows its specific historical efficacy" (Sahlins 1985:xiv). An event is thus an emic construal of an etic phenomenon.

To further open the problem of the fashioning of history to our view, Sahlins "interposes" the "structure of the conjuncture" between structures and events: "By the 'structure of the conjuncture' I mean the practical realization of the cultural categories in a historical context, as expressed in the interested action of the historic agents, including the microsociology of the interaction" (1985:xiv). The structure of the conjuncture, then, is the arena in which history is meaningfully assembled. It is where coherent frames of the past are brought to bear on the ambiguities and general lack of fit of the present.

The concept of the structure of the conjuncture allows us to address the discrepancy between outsiders' perceptions of discontinuity and Chilcotin people's sense of continuity between past and present. It also gives us methodological purpose. It directs us toward situations and practices in which people shape the present, and in a sense advance themselves, by enveloping the flux of unfolding experience within the frameworks available in memories. These frameworks turn out to be structures of voices, past and present, brought into active relation with one another in narrative practice. Thus, there is a sense in which pursuing the structure of the conjuncture requires in turn that we reaffirm our commitment to the ethnography of speaking, albeit in a modified form.

To sum up the theoretical approach, this is an event-centered study of the use of "traditional" verbal genres as "the interactional practices of 'traditional life'" themselves framed within the ethnography of communication and the anthropology of history. It is an attempt to contend with the growing complexity of the pragmatics of historical genres (analysis of such being exemplified in a growing body of works: Basso 1979, 1996; Bauman 1986; Briggs and Bauman 1999; Cruikshank 1998; Darnell 1974; Dinwoodie 1999; Hanks 1986, 1987; Hill 1995; Hymes 1981; Moore 1993, 2000; Parks and De-Mallie 1992; Silverstein 1996a) in the context of rapid economic and historical change (as characterized in Brody 1988; Collins 1998; Hill 1985, 1986; Silverstein 1996b; Wolf 1982). It is a study of the reaccentuation of traditional genres and a study of "how the new event genres are assimilated in some respects to local 'traditional' forms" (Silverstein 1998:411).

The Circumstances Surrounding the Research

This research was initiated while I was a graduate student at the University of Chicago (1986–96), though the impulse to study something like this developed much earlier. Interest in the area was kindled during my introduction to the Salish and neighboring languages in college courses with Dr. Anthony Mattina at the University of Montana. Dr. Mattina conveyed to me the extraordinary formal intricacies of Native languages, something of the remarkable fortitude of the speakers who had preserved these languages, and the urgency of documenting the rich array of Native American linguistic practices. I applied to graduate school in hopes of continuing my studies in these areas. My interest in central British Columbia increased as I learned more about it in coursework with Raymond Fogelson and Michael Silverstein.

I first traveled to the Williams Lake area of British Columbia in the summer of 1989 to establish connections with the relevant tribal governments. The next summer I returned to the area and initiated formal study of the language with the expert assistance of Georgina Johnny of Toosey Reserve. I rented a room in a (as it turned out, condemned) house in Williams Lake and drove out to Toosey Reserve for each session of linguistic work, returning to town in the evenings.

With the assistance of a Wenner-Gren dissertation grant, I initiated formal doctoral research in 1991. Many had suggested that the Nemiah Valley Indian Band was most likely to support my research, so I drove there directly from Chicago in September 1991. Fortunately, they took me in and set me up in a reserve house on the condition that I help with some research projects of their own (see chapter 2). Broke, in late spring (April) I returned to Chicago in hopes of finding more support. I acquired a dean's fellowship and returned for three more months in fall 1992. I returned again for a month in summer 1993. I defended a dissertation based on that work in fall 1995. I returned to Nemiah Valley in the summers of 1997, 1998, 1999, 2000 and the current work represents a version of the dissertation reworked on the basis of subsequent experience.

The resulting book is organized as follows. The historical, geographic, linguistic, and social contexts required for understanding contemporary life at Nemiah Valley Indian Reserve are presented in chapter 1. Though it has maintained a considerable degree of local integrity to this day, the fur trade (coastal and interior sectors) and the agricultural development that accompanied the British Columbian gold rush of the 1850s and 1860s both influenced life at Nemiah Valley. Ranching was taken up by most Chilcotin families and today is considered to be a traditional activity. Nowadays, logging, mining, and tourism are growing in significance within the local economy. Along with economic diversification has come an increase in the complexity of communication. Several varieties of English are now spoken along with a full range of Chilcotin registers. These various linguistic varieties, in Bakhtin's words, "mutually reveal each other's presence and [have] beg[u]n to function for each other as dialogizing backgrounds" (1981:414).

Historical narrative practice as I experienced it is described in chapter 2. Historical narratives are typically presented at the margins of public events, which these days are for the most part "conducted" by outsiders. The telling of such narratives forces participants to rethink the principles underlying such events and, ultimately, the underlying forces shaping history in the modern world.

Myths are presented in a more select range of occasions than historical narratives these days. They are more rarely heard. However, on certain occasions people reflect on the possible relations between mythical scenarios and the happenstances of their lives. An instance of this, which culminated in the presentation of a mythological narrative, is documented and analyzed in chapter 3.

Recently, First Nations peoples have been exploring the rhetorical resources available for use in the public sphere. When the Nemiah Valley Indian Band somewhat reluctantly began to fight against those who would clear-cut their traditional lands, they issued a declaration. The band is not opposed to logging but, rather, to the style of industrial clear-cutting that effectively forecloses on any future uses of an area. Out of necessity the band leadership appropriated the rhetorical form of the declaration to address the international public. While this might seem to represent the adoption of a new form of political discourse, a closer look shows that the fundamental rhetorical template of the "new discourse" comes from the oldest discourse known to the group.

By way of concluding, various approaches that underlie this study are summarized and evaluated for the contributions they make. It is very difficult to orient oneself analytically in the present without some theoretical reference to political economy. Nonetheless, now more than ever, observing anything but the commonplaces of inexorable global change requires devoting systematic attention to local practices and local values. A modified version of the ethnography of speaking is well suited to the task.

1. Ethnographic Contexts

This construction cannot be completely understood at a remove
from the conditions of its social realization.
M. M. Bakhtin and P. N. Medvedev (1968)

In the main this book consists of descriptions and interpretations of specific occasions of narrative practice. This chapter is an exception. The aim of the chapter is to sketch the historical, political, linguistic, and social contexts that activate and are activated by historical narratives of various kinds.

Historical Background

The Nemiah Valley Indian community—members call themselves Xeni Gwet'in (people of the valley of Xeni)—is a group of roughly 350 Indian people living on the Nemiah Valley Indian Reserve in west-central British Columbia, Canada. The reserve is one of six or seven, depending on how one counts, that constitute what anthropologists have called the Chilcotin Tribe. Many reserve members now consider themselves members of the Tsilhqut'in (Chilcotin) or Xeni Gwet'in First Nation.

The area in which all reserves of the tribe are situated is known among non-Indians as the Chilcotin. The Chilcotin region is a plateau that slopes from the Fraser River up into the rugged Coastal Range to the west. The western part of the area is timbered with lodgepole pine, spruce, ponderosa, and Douglas fir and features an occasional meadow. The eastern part consists of meadows broken up by stands of spruce, lodgepole, and poplar. The west consists of evergreen forest and lakes. The east is relatively dry.

Archaeological evidence corresponds to the view of contemporary elders by suggesting that a distinctively Chilcotin cultural pattern has existed along the Chilcotin River for well over 500 years (Wilmeth 1978). Over time, archaeologists infer, the Chilcotin have moved from the Eagle Lake area east down the river to areas once occupied by Interior Salish peoples. Archaeological evidence makes Chilcotin claims of long-term inhabitance in the area intelligible and legally defensible.

The permanence of their ties to the area was reinforced by the systematic nature of the seasonal cycle. In winter time people camped on medium-sized lakes, where *dek'any* 'trout,' *sabay* 'Dolly Varden,' *lhos'esch'el* 'whitefish,' and *tatsesh* 'suckers,' could be netted under the ice with some regularity (see Tyhurst). Small parties would routinely depart on short trips to hunt for *mus* 'moose,' *nists'i* 'deer,' and *didiny* 'marmots' and to trap for *tsa* 'beaver,' *nabi* 'muskrat,' and *dlik* 'squirrel.' If the snow was not too deep, people would also pick herbs like *bedzish ts'ediyan* 'labrador tea' in lower marshy areas.

When necessary the diet was supplemented with *ts'aman* 'sockeye salmon' dried the previous summer and fall.

In spring people followed the line of melting snow up into higher country. This was the most difficult time of year. Supplies of dried fish and dried roots were low. The ice on the lakes was soft, and people could fall through easily. The ground was wet and muddy. Temperatures were higher than in winter, but because of the water it was harder to stay warm. Travel was difficult because of high rivers and snow-choked passes.

Moving steadily up with the large game, people would arrive in the high country in early summer to gather *suntiny* 'spring beauty' (*Claytonia lanceolata*) and *ʔesghunsh* 'avalanche lily' (*Erythronium grandiflorum*). The roots, or corms, were located by their blossoms. Because the blossoms wilt as spring turns into summer, a premium was placed on arriving early in the high country. Corms were dug up and eaten, and some were dried for later use. *Didiny* 'marmots,' *dibi* 'mountain sheep,' *sebay* 'mountain goats,' and *nists'i* 'deer' were hunted and eaten, and their hides were tanned. As the salmon began to run people would come down from the mountains to camp along the rivers, netting and drying as much salmon as possible for the coming winter and gathering *dig* 'Saskatoon berries' and *nelgus* 'chokecherries.'

In early fall, people would once again move up to the higher elevations to hunt the by now fat game and pick *nelghes* 'wild blueberries,' *texaltsel* 'wild raspberries,' *ʔundziny* 'wild strawberries,' *nuwaish* 'soapberries,' and *dig*, among others. When the weather required, people would again descend to the lakes, and the cycle would begin again.

An integral dimension of the traditional pattern, it seems, involved transporting hides and horns from the high country in late fall over the mountains to the Bella Coola. Such journeys were frequently followed by lengthy visits, with people sometimes staying for entire winters. Food, lodging, and goodwill could be purchased with desirables such as mountain goat horns and various assorted hides. In addition, the Chilcotin could contribute to Coastal life by serving as enthusiastic and appreciative audience members for winter ceremonies.

The Chilcotin area first attracted the attention of Europeans when explorer and fur trader Alexander MacKenzie traveled across the northern portion on his journey to the Pacific Ocean in 1793. Shortly thereafter the area was engulfed in two sectors of the fur trade. Systematic land-based trade began in the interior of British Columbia with the merger of the Northwest Company and the Hudson Bay Company in 1821 (Wolf 1982:182). With the establishment of Fort Alexander and Fort Chilcotin (1829–44), the easternmost bands of the Chilcotin were brought into the interior trade.

At roughly the same time—"by the 1830s the sea otter had become scarce, and [coastal] trade shifted from the islanders to the mainlanders" (Wolf 1982:189)—the westernmost band of the Tsilhqut'in became involved with the coastal trade. The effects of the fur trade extended well into the hinterlands of the Chilcotin. For example, to control inland fur supplies, mainland (Coastal) groups extended their kinship networks:

> In these relations between coastal groups and groups in the hinterland, kin ties often structured the partnership of asymmetrical trade. The Bella Coola, for example, integrated the Alkatcho Carrier into their network of trade partners by accepting Alkatcho men as sons-in-law. These Alkatcho affinals were recruited from "the successful hunters, the shrewd and energetic traders, the lucky gamblers" (Goldman 1940:344)—those who were able to furnish their Bella Coola fathers-in-law with furs. In turn, they obtained noble Bella Coola wives, as well as titles and big names from the wife-giving lineage. As a result, there developed an Alkatcho "aristocracy," which became enmeshed in the Bella Coola potlatch system. The most important Alkatcho "noble" of a village became its potlatch chief and its agent in inter-village potlatches. The real authority of such figures remained limited, however. The Alkatcho subsistence base was too restricted to permit any but minor potlatch exchanges; "an ordinary exchange involved some ten blankets" (Goldman 1940:347). Property was destroyed among the Bella Coola, but among the Alkatcho it was only symbolically "thrown into the fire." Potlatching increased the productivity of the extended families that participated and led some Alkatcho entrepreneurs to collect furs from neighboring Carrier and Chilcotin, but the restricted productive base ultimately set limits to the escalation of potlatching. The Alkatcho, furthermore, did not take over the elaborate secret society complex of their wealthier affinals. The failure to adopt these forms may have been, in part, the result of difficulty in supporting such events with the humble resources of the Alkatcho villages. At the same time, the Bella Coola guarded these ceremonials and the associated ritual prerogatives as ways of impressing their neighbors, who also remained fearful of Bella Coola sorcery. (Wolf 1982:189–190, emphasis added)

The Shuswap to the east also sought trade with the Chilcotin. Thus, Chilcotin could move their products—hides for the most part—in both directions. As trade developed they also moved dentalia and other coastal goods across the plateau to their eastern neighbors, and they moved guns and horses west to their coastal neighbors.

Gold was discovered along the Fraser River in 1858. At the time no mining was done in the Chilcotin per se, but ranchers began to flood in to supply the growing need for food in the burgeoning mining communities. As they tried to appropriate springs and other scarce resources in the 1860s, conflicts began to increase. In some cases the result was fighting; in others, agreement. Over time, the Chilcotin became as heavily involved in the economic and kinship-based networks of the ranching industry as they had been in the fur trade.

The geographical isolation of the Chilcotin—because of the Fraser River canyon on the east and the formidable coastal mountains to the west— constrained other forms of development, and cattle ranching dominated the local economy until recently. Logging began in earnest when the river was spanned with steel bridges in the 1960s. Subsequently, mining and tourism came to the area as well. Today logging is the dominant industry, with tourism and mining growing in importance, but small-scale ranching has continued to play a part to this day.

Contemporary Reserves

At roughly 1,200 residents, Anaham (Tl'etinqux) is the largest contemporary Tsilhqut'in reserve. It is located along the middle portion of the Chilcotin River more or less in the heart of Tsilhqut'in country. Anaham was formed when people living in the timber and lakes environment of the western Chilcotin moved east to the flat, grassy meadows of the middle Chilcotin in the fur trading and early ranching period. Later, the French missionary order known as the Oblates of Mary Immaculate (founded in 1812 by Eugene de Mazenod as a small elite order for the purpose of reinvigorating the priesthood in the wake the antichurch policies of Napoleon [Whitehead 1981]) established the main Chilcotin mission and school at Anaham.

The meadows along the Chilcotin River have been owned by non-Indian ranchers for as long as anyone can remember. The area north and west of the reserve is largely public land under provincial jurisdiction known as Crown land. Williams Lake, the urban center of central British Columbia, is forty minutes from Anaham by car.

Located roughly five miles southeast on a dirt road, on the other side of the Chilcotin River, is Stoney Reserve (home of the Gaxnedzenaghilht'in). With a population of roughly 400, Stoney is a compact, tight-knit community, considered by some more ideologically conservative than Anaham.

Redstone Reserve (Tsideldel) is located fifty miles west of Anaham in a series of meadows bordered by sandstone bluffs. Houses are laid out on several blocks of rectilinear streets surrounding the Band Office. Other houses are scattered around the neighboring hills. In recent years effective leadership has made Redstone one of the most economically dynamic of Chilcotin communities.

Roughly fifty miles further west of Redstone, making it 100 miles west of contemporary Anaham, is the original Anaham community (Nagwentl'un), now known as the Anahim Lake community (note the spelling difference). Some Chilcotin people still live there along with Carrier people and others. The population of Chilcotin at Anahim has dwindled to roughly fifty, depending on how people identify themselves. Despite the mix, the small numbers, and the fact that it is typically not represented in gatherings of Tsilhqut'in (Chilcotin) National Government leaders, people sometimes explicitly include it among the Chilcotin communities.

Twenty miles east of Stoney and Anaham—which is to say, twenty miles closer to the town of Williams Lake—is Toosey Reserve (Tl'esqux). Many members of the Toosey Band have relatives among the Shuswap peoples who now live along the Fraser River to the east. Houses are more spread out than at reserves other than Nemiah. The band has about the same number of people as Stoney. Toosey has less access to a traditional resource base than the other Chilcotin reserves and has come to be somewhat more dependent on Williams Lake. Although most have learned trades (e.g., stone engraving, mechanics), people at Toosey are concerned with continuing their traditional ways. For example, they make the most of their proximity to the river and energetically maximize their access to local fishing sites.

On the west side of the Fraser River near the once hub of the fur trade, Fort Alexanderia, is Marguerite Reserve (ʔesdilagh). The residents at Marguerite are Chilcotin, Carrier, and Shuswap. As in the case of Anahim Lake, Chilcotin identity remains important, though many people also identify themselves as Carrier or Shuswap.

The Nemiah Valley Indian Reserve (Xeni) is furthest from town, located in the southwest regions of the Chilcotin area. It is set in a small east–west valley that opens to the fifty-mile-long Chilko Lake to the west and rugged foothills and the glacier-fed Tazeko River to the east, where considerable hunting and gathering resources are still available. There is one small store in the valley, located just off the reserve itself, which sells candy bars, frozen hamburgers, raffle tickets, and a few pairs of blue jeans.

Grossly oversimplifying, Toosey Reserve is most oriented to contemporary Canadian culture, by necessity, and also to neighboring Shuswap culture and ranching. Anaham has been most influenced by the Oblate order of the Catholic Church. Adjacent to the historic Chilko Ranch, Stoney is home to a large number of working cowboys. Marguerite is most connected to the legacy of the fur trade.

A sketch of reserve life would be inadequate without some mention of what is common to all. Ranching holds a special place in the lives of Chilcotin people of all reserves. On every reserve are found remarkable ranching families, and over the course of the year everyone gets involved in one way or another. Nemiah Valley stands out as the most "traditional" reserve because of the availability of natural resources. Most families continue to run cattle and hunt, gather, and fish on the Crown lands surrounding Nemiah Valley. As elsewhere, traditional activities are mixed with contracts for fencing, timber thinning, firewood cutting, house construction, and such service-type contract work as road grading.

The Speech Community

Prior to the fur trade Chilcotin speech communities were essentially local in character. Chilcotin social organization was relatively egalitarian, and for the most part communication was limited to face-to-face social contacts. The Chilcotin language served as the basis of communication within and between families and in subsistence activities. Anecdotal evidence suggests that the Chilcotin have been required to use the languages of their interlocutors when trading or interacting with other groups. Multilingualism in Chilcotin and Shuswap was present among members of eastern bands; multilingualism in Chilcotin and Bella Coola, among the western; and multilingualism in Chilcotin and Carrier, among the northern. While several languages were present in the area, most activities were conducted in Chilcotin, the "vernacular" or "local language" (Gumperz 1964:420, 1968:466–468).

With the fur trade, missionization, and ranching came the "argots" of Chinook Jargon and English. Though no systematic research has been done, it seems that they were not put to general use. These linguistic varieties seem to have been used only in those new realms of activity. Many individuals became sufficiently adept to serve as go-betweens, though the number of people fully proficient in either seems to have been proportionately small. By contrast to the case for the Shuswap people, for example, virtually no administrative opportunities seem to have been extended to Chilcotin people in forts or missions. No doubt there were exceptions, but generally speaking, the Chilcotin were not centrally involved in the social institutions that grew to encompass the greater Pacific Northwest. As a result, Chilcotin speakers continued to rely on their native vernacular long after other groups began shifting toward the general use of Chinook Jargon, French, or English.

Today the linguistic situation is more complex because the communities have become more complex. For example, the Department of Indian Affairs now administers all its major programs through local leaders. An ever growing cadre of Chilcotin people is involved in politics, social work, accounting, forestry, and so forth. The Department of Indian Affairs uses English as the administrative code. With the closing of the Oblate mission school in the 1970s, most Chilcotin children began attending public schools. Courses in Native language and history were instituted at the time, and in the Chilcotin area Chilcotin individuals were hired to teach them. Several women who attended the public schools in the 1970s and 1980s went on to gain degrees in education at the University of British Columbia. They returned to local public schools to teach and help administer the general curriculum. The public schools, too, use English as their administrative code.

Like leaders from other Native communities, then, Chilcotin leaders have now become centrally involved in a new regional economic and social system. This involvement has stratified the Chilcotin community so that in certain respects it has come to resemble what once were called "intermediate societies" (Gumperz 1968:461; see also Casagrande 1959:1; Cohn and Marriott 1958:1). In contrast to "tribal societies," Gumperz has observed, intermediate societies "tend to show loyalty to [linguistic] codes which may be quite distinct from the vernacular" (1968:469). The considerable social distance that has opened up between those who administer programs and those who partake of them is an a sense measured and marked by the considerable grammatical difference between the varieties of English and Chilcotin prevalent today.

In other respects, however, the community is showing signs of standardization within the Canadian national system. Public school is playing a greater and greater role in the community. Identifying with the social milieu of public school, students of today seem to have a deeper psychological relationship to English than their parents and even than those who now use it routinely as an administrative code. The idea of Canadian English as standard is reinforced in job prerequisites, in radio and television broadcasts, and in the increasingly frequent exposure to the Canadian linguistic economy from journeys to Vancouver and beyond. Of great interest to all at Nemiah Valley is the recent institution of a Chilcotin-immersion program for the kindergarten portion of the Naghtaneked public school at Nemiah Valley. Whatever the effect on the vitality of the Chilcotin language, interest in the program has certainly further confirmed local commitment to public schooling.

Today, most Chilcotin people speak Chilcotin and English. Whether English or Chilcotin dominates varies from reserve to reserve and from context to context, though among elders the situation is fairly uniform. All men and women above the age of roughly fifty speak Chilcotin, and most prefer it. It is uncommon for elders to speak fluent English, and though there are prominent exceptions, it is uncommon for female elders to speak English at all. Many members of this group attended boarding school for at least a few years and are at least partially literate in English. Few read novels or newspapers. Most enjoy reading catalogs. No elders are literate in Chilcotin, a point of mild consternation in the community at large.

Nearly everyone between the ages of thirty and fifty is bilingual. On such reserves as Nemiah Valley, Redstone, and Stoney, and among the families living off reserve at Puntzi and Eagle Lake, people in this age group speak Chilcotin regularly and comfortably, if not always up to the standards of their elders. On such reserves as Anaham, Marguerite, and Toosey, and among those now living in town, people in this age group predominantly speak English. Virtually all members of this group everywhere in Chilcotin country are at least passively fluent in Chilcotin. Minimally, they understand fairly complex discourse produced by others and respond effectively but have limited ability to initiate Chilcotin discourse. Most people in this young adult category are literate in English. Despite the limited nature of their Chilcotin-speaking abilities, a significant portion of them are partially literate in Chilcotin as a result of either attending school, helping to teach Chilcotin language and history, or working with linguists.

Everyone younger than thirty years old speaks English. Some speakers are recognized to be especially proficient in Chilcotin, and some are clearly dependent on Chilcotin whether they are recognized to be good speakers or not. Others exhibit English-dominant bilingualism. Everyone who is originally from Nemiah Valley to my knowledge is at least passively fluent. Some who come in from other reserves are passively familiar, if not exactly fluent.

While these are impressionistic descriptions and would be difficult to justify in any systematic way, they give some sense of the range of abilities of speakers. Considerable variation is evident, but a couple of general observations can be made. Even of speakers who exhibit considerable grammatical control, it is often remarked that "they do not speak their own language." Those in politically marginal families tend to be evaluated as the poorest speakers of English, and despite outsiders' impression that they use Chilcotin more consistently, they are not necessarily viewed as "better" speakers within the community. Men and women below the age of thirty often speak English among peers. Where the native language is strongest, members of this age group can communicate effectively in Chilcotin when required, as when speaking to or in the presence of elders and perhaps when speaking among peers away from the reserve. Where the language is weaker, members of this age group have limited control of speaking and are not confident about comprehension. All social sectors are familiar with the language, and yet in no quarter is it entirely secure. Even at conservative reserves such as Nemiah Valley, there are indications of language shift, such as the frequent to preponderant use of English among some sectors in some situations and the fact that only a few younger people are singled out as having particularly strong control of their native language.

Social Organization

Chilcotin social organization was based on three sorts of groups: encampments, families, and bands. Prior to the formation of reserve communities, "the main cooperating" groups seem to have been what Robert Lane calls "encampments" (what the Chilcotin called *qwentux* '[clusters of] houses'). Encampments were "unnamed local groups" consisting of members of "several families who usually, particularly in the winter time, camped together":

> Several brothers and their families might form such a group; or parents and their families, and their children and their families. Several friends might form such a group and through intermarriage between the friends' families, the unity of the group would be perpetuated. In another case, a family might join with others because of its inability to shift for itself, because of the death or handicap of one of the parents, or because of laziness.
>
> In these encampments there was a great deal of mobility. A family might remain in such an association for a season or a lifetime. Probably most families had constituted parts of several different local groups in the course of their existence. (Lane 1953:170)

Families sometimes represented genealogical subdivisions within encampments; other times, they represented genealogical linkages between encampments. Whereas encampments were defined primarily on the basis of coresidence, families were defined partly on the basis of genealogy. In principle families extended outward indefinitely because kinship (see below) was figured bilaterally. Nevertheless, residence seems to have been one important principle for limiting family membership, and in many cases encampments consisted of single families. Notwithstanding the fact that people defined the family genealogically in some circumstances, when people speak of "family" they often imagine a definite, delimited, local group, which was part of an encampment or which represented a minimal encampment. Thus the term was sometimes used to represent a sort of minimal local group.

Bands embraced sets of related encampments. Though they seem to have come together "only upon a few special occasions such as feasts and celebrations" (Lane 1953:172), bands represented salient frames of reference for individuals. Bands were named—generally "for the lake with which [they] were most intimately associated" (Lane 1953:166)—and they mediated people's relations to territory:

> In theory membership in the band depended only upon the fact of common territorial occupation. There was a degree of difference in feeling toward and behavior toward those born and raised in the band territory and those who move into it. Attitudes towards the latter were somewhat ambivalent insofar as the whole of the band was concerned. This is explained by the process by which one changed band affiliation. A person or family did not move into a new band or territory in which it lacked some connections, friends or relatives. These ties, which were to individuals, determined the reception of new band members. If a person had many such ties, more of the whole band would welcome him; but the fewer the ties (almost anyone would have a few since the total population was small) the smaller the welcome would be and the smaller the degree of identification of the new settler with the band and of the band with the new settler. The majority of families in a band were closely related by descent or marriage. (Lane 1953:167)

Membership, then, in bands, encampments, and families was shaped by both genealogy and residence, each depending in part on the other. The fusion of the two seems to have given Chilcotin bands, encampments, and families a degree of corporateness associated with descent groups.

The corporateness of Chilcotin groups was also a function, in my estimation, of their participation in a wide range of regional relations. The purely kindred-based forms of organization characteristic of their northern Athabaskan hunting heritage were elaborated under both the influence of neighbors with definitive corporate groups and regular interactions among Chilcotin encampments as were instigated by their geographic positioning between sectors of coastal and interior trade as noted above. Bands regularly traded and married among themselves and among their neighbors. Without accepting Elman Service's evolutionary model, we can still use his comments regarding the cline of band organization to clarify Chilcotin social organization:

> The band . . . may take its definition merely from the fact that its members feel closely enough related that they do not intermarry. In some instances they also define themselves territorially, as in-

habitants and "owners" of a foraging range. In other cases, joint totemic or ceremonial meetings help set them apart. In any event, marriages which set up or intensify relationships with other bands reciprocally tend to distinguish bands more clearly from one another. (1966:7)

Evidence suggests that the Chilcotin defined themselves on both genealogical and territorial grounds. Indeed, as Service suggests it might, intermarriage seems to have enhanced the identity of bands.

The idea of customary use was central to Chilcotin notions of territorial ownership. For example, "it was recognized that the families in [encampments] had rights to certain winter camping sites, providing that they occupied them every season. There were no strong rules about this; it would be impolite and would breed ill feeling were someone else to 'jump the claim.' However, when the usual occupants of such a site failed to use it for one or more winters, someone else could move in and claim it" (Lane 1953:171). Memories are long, however, and in cases I am familiar with families have used the idea of customary use to retain at least partial claims to an area decades after any actual use or inhabitance.

Four kinds of leaders figure in the Chilcotin literature (for more on leadership, see chapter 3): informal activities leaders, potlatch big men, shamans, and chiefs. Informal activities leaders were those who took initiative in encampment-based projects such as building fish weirs. This form of leadership was apparently partly determined by the nature of the project, but "a limited group of abler men was accorded respect as leaders" (Lane 1953:206) across a wide range of activities.

Potlatch big man status required the giving of four feasts over the course of several years. The man who could muster enough surplus for such ceremonial feasting was then known in the Chilcotin language as *nidziⱭin*. Lane speculates that the "formalization of the *nidziⱭin*-ship with the ceremonial validation of the title may be due to recent influences ultimately from the Coast" (1953:207).

Diyen 'powers/empowered,' or shamans, were distinguished by having supernatural helpers (Lane 1953:208). They had special abilities to intervene in matters of sorcery and warfare. Lane indicates that shamans were often also recognized as political leaders. This form of leadership is characteristic of the Chilcotin's northern Athabaskan hunting relatives.

Last, band chiefs were instituted after contact and eventually formalized by the Department of Indian Affairs. Nowadays, men and women are appointed "chiefs" according to Department of Indian Affairs protocol, which generally speaking, is based on popular election. For the most part "chiefs" are elected on the basis of the perception that they can effectively engage the wider world, and that perception is based primarily on English proficiency.

Marriage and Kinship

Four principles guide Chilcotin marriages: personal compatibility, status, residence, and genealogy. First, people prefer the company of some individuals over that of others. Personal affection plays a significant part in people's decisions regarding marriage.

Second, while the differences are not pronounced, some families have more status than others. Status seems to be based on family wealth and power. Members of relatively high status families tend to marry members of other high-status families, though given that the differences are not clear-cut, this is a relatively weak pattern.

Third, according to the principle of residence, Chilcotin people prefer to marry in the same area. Fourth, according the principle of genealogy, Chilcotin people prefer to marry outside of their extended families. The principles of residence and genealogy overlap to generate three types of marriage. The first type of marriage results when people stay in their home areas by marrying distant relatives such as cousins. The very slight degree of impropriety is generally overlooked in the community. Such marriages, however, are generally not confirmed in church rituals. The second type of marriage results when people marry out of their families by marrying into adjacent Chilcotin or Shuswap communities. Such couples generally face more travel time between families, but such marriages are more prestigious than the first type. The third type of marriage results when people are able to find suitable partners in their own home areas who happen to not be relatives. This is the most highly esteemed form of marriage, though it is relatively uncommon. Such marriages are almost always celebrated with full church formalities.

When a person died, the tradition was to disperse their property. It was dispersed in four ways. First, some was "sent" with the deceased. Favorite horses, dogs, clothes, and tools, for example, were often buried or burned with the deceased. Second, the cattle of the deceased would be slaughtered by the family as an offering to all who attended and assisted with the funeral. Third, some horses or cattle were given away as the prize in the stick games that followed the funeral services. Only nonrelatives could play in such games. Fourth, remaining clothing and possessions were destroyed. In consequence, nothing was passed on in such a way as to maintain descent groups. In principle at least no one inherited anything but rights to use certain territories. While the pattern has changed somewhat to accommodate Western ideas of property, the traditional ideal is maintained in people's minds.

Table 1: Kinship Terminology

Consanguines

+2	-ci	FF, MF	-cu	FM, MM				
	ʾinci	(voc)	ʾincu	(voc)				

+1	-ta	F	-ban	M	-zʾai	FB, MB	-biz	FZ, MZ
	ʾaba	(voc)	ʾinkwel	(voc)				

0	-nagh	OB	-di	oZ	-lhtes	MBD, MBS, FZD, FZS
	-chel	yB	-diz	yZ		

-1	-yi	s (m)	-yaz	s (f)	-c'oi	'nephew'
	-cai	D (m)	-yac'i	(f)	-zi	'niece'

-2	-cui	SS, SD, DS, DD (m)		-chai	SS, SD, DS, DD (f)

Affines

+1	ʾetsiyan	F-in-law	ʾitu	M-in-law

0	(-) qen	Husband	jighandan	B-in-law
	(-) ʾad	Wife	ʾeghi	z-in-law

-1	ʾiyasʾad	D-in-law

The Chilcotin kinship terminology is essentially Iroquoian (see table 1). The two terms of reference in the second ascending generation, *-ci* FF, MF, and *-cu* FM, MM, cover the grandparents on the mother's and father's sides. A second set of terms, *ʾinci* FF, MF, and *ʾincu* MM, FM, is used for address.

There are four terms of reference in the first ascending generation: *-ta* F, *-ban* M, *-zʾi* FB, MB, and *-biz* FZ, MZ. Specific terms are used for the address of mother (*ʾinkwel*) and father (*ʾaba*), but all of the mother's siblings and all of the father's siblings are treated the same way.

In ego's generation there are five terms of reference: *-nagh* OB, *-chel* yB, *-di* oZ, *-diz* yZ, and *-lhtes* MBS, MBD, FZS, FZD. Sibling terms are applied to siblings per se and to parallel cousins. A separate term, *-lhtes* MBS, MBD, FZS, FZD, is used to designate cross cousins.

Six terms of reference are present in the first descending generation: *-yi* S (male possr), *-yaz* S (female possr), *-cai* D (male possr), *-yac'i* D (female possr), *-c'oy* BS, ZS, *-zi* BD, ZD. It is noteworthy that these terms vary depending on whether the possessor is male or female. In practice this means that husbands and wives generally refer to and address their children differently.

In the second descending generation, like the second ascending, there are two terms, *-cui* SS, SD, DS, DD (male possr), and *-chai* SS, SD, DS, DD (female possr). However, the terms in this case differentiate the sex of the possessor rather than the sex of the referent.

Affinal terms including *(-)qen* 'husband' and *(-)ʾaed* 'wife' are used frequently. Others, including *-tsiyan* 'F-in-law,' *-ʾitu* 'M-in-law,' *jighandan* 'B-in-law,' *ʾeghai* 'Z-in-law,' and *ʾiyasʾad* 'D-in-law,' are heard less often.

Behaviors Signifying Kinship

In addition to the use of kinship terms there are other ways in which the underlying realities of families and family relations are attested. For example, elders often address members of other families by the name of the most important ancestor of that extended family, as though in meeting this person the elders are encountering the other family writ small. When I first noticed elders addressing other elders this way, I interpreted it is a style of deferring to peers by using the names of their parents or grandparents. But then I also observed elders addressing younger people in this way. At a glance this resembles the use of surnames when one might expect first names, given that the ancestors in question generally are the source of family surnames. However, the use of surnames is very recent at Nemiah Valley and generally follows the Canadian practice of women giving up their surnames upon marriage. Moreover, surnames are anglicized. When people mean to designate an ancestor, they always employ Tsilhqut'in pronunciation. This is a complicated act when considered from the point of view of semiotics. A person present to the senses is seen to stand for a family, in a form of synecdoche. Simultaneously, an ancestor is understood to stand for the family. The second synecdoche is then activated to stand in place of the first, resulting in what we might characterize as an inverted indexical synecdoche! This is achieved, of course, with no discernable cognitive distress.

Second, on formal occasions the community sometimes represents the relations among families iconically, in patterns reminiscent of Lévi-Strauss's famous discussions of South American social organization (see 1963). For example, at a marriage being held outdoors at the rodeo grounds at Nemiah Valley, I noticed that everyone had parked in a circle with their vehicles pointing inward. I quickly noticed that family members had parked next to other family members. People stayed in their vehicles for a time talking with those in adjacent vehicles and observing others across the way (some using binoculars). Only when I spoke with a friend and he observed, "We park

Table 2. Ethnonyms of the Chilcotin and Surrounding Peoples

Chilcotin Bands

Tsilhqut'in	'people of the Chilko River'
Xeni gwet'in	'people of Nemiah Valley'
Gaxnets'enaghilht'i gwet'in	'people of Stoney Reserve'
Tl'et'inqut'in	'people of Anaham'
Tl'esqut'in	'people of Toosey [lit., people of muddy creek]'
ʔest'elagh	'people of Marguerite'
Tsideldel gwet'in	'people of Redstone'

Carrier Bands

ts'ut'in	'Burns Lake Carrier'
ʔenchat'in	'people of Anahim Lake'
nichat'in	'people of Kluskus'
ʔalhgachugh	'people of Algatcho'

Salish Communities

ʔesch'ed	'people of Lillooet'
qaju	'people of Bute Inlet (North Coast Salish)'
ʔena	'Northern Shuswap; strangers'
ʔenaghi	'people of Bella Coola'

Peoples, Native Peoples

dení	'Human beings, Chilcotin people'
nenqayni	'Chilcotin people, Indians, [lit. earth surface people]'

Non-Indians

midugh	'non-Chilcotin, non-Indians'
baghasten	'American (*Boston*, Chinook Jargon)'
dzaman	'Chinese (*Chinaman*)'
nigel	'Africans'

where we live," did I notice that the spatial arrangement of people evident in the parking pattern served as a sort of abstract representation of where familial groups reside relative to one another. In other words, the arrangement served as an indexical icon of family territory in relation to the community as a whole.

In these and in an open-ended number of other ways the underlying realities of families and family relations are expressed and affirmed. Notwithstanding changes, families and family relations continue to serve as the primary touchstones for social reality at Nemiah.

Ethnonyms

Robert Lane (1953) reported the use of a variety of names for surrounding peoples, and the terms are all still in use. I list them in table 2, more or less from those most closely related to those most distant. These ethnonyms terms illustrate the cultural codification of a wide array of ethnic relationships.

Conclusion

The limited evidence suggests that participation in the fur trade consolidated a role for Chilcotin peoples as intermediaries between coast and interior, between the French and Crees of trading companies and the Athabaskan and Salish peoples. The ranching and mission era brought further intensification of ethnic relations, this time primarily with Canadians of Anglo-American and British extraction. With growing participation in Canadian national programs, the linguistic situation has grown in complexity. Today the Chilcotin speech community appears to be shifting toward the use of English, though the shift is not uniform, and considerable loyalty to the native language remains. The salient groups on the ground have changed to a degree with government policies, but kinship relations appear to be consistent. The picture that emerges is one of cultural integrity (not the same thing as stasis) in the face of long- and short-term economic change.

2. Historical Narrative

The genre guides its speaker to the theme of the tragedy.
Melville Jacobs (1968)

I met William Abraham shortly after I first arrived at Nemiah Valley in 1991. At the time William was about sixty-five years old. He wore pointed-toe cowboy boots, Wrangler jeans, a wide belt, a snap-button shirt, and a new yellow Caterpillar cap—all as neat as though they had just come from the dry cleaners. His salt-and-pepper hair was cut close on the sides. Though no longer young, William still walked with a snap in his step. His posture was straight, and his expression alert.

He was staying the night with his wife Mary in an otherwise unoccupied cabin at the east end of Konni Lake, at a place known by the Chilcotin people of Nemiah Valley as Naghatanaqed 'where the waves wash up.' William and Marie were traveling by horse-drawn wagon from their permanent home on the reserve at the west end of Nemiah Valley up to an area in the high country called Naghbas (after a mountain, called Obsidian [Mountain]), southeast of the valley. He hoped to check on his cows, scout for game, and reacquaint himself with the place.

I had come to the valley only a few days before. I was hoping to begin research for a dissertation study of genealogy and place at Nemiah Valley. Studying the Chilcotin language at Toosey Reserve the summer before, I had resolved to do fieldwork at Nemiah Valley, where, by all accounts, the community was likely to support such research. I had had no luck raising mail correspondence with the Nemiah Valley Indian Band, and there was only one radiotelephone in the valley. So I had simply driven out in an old navy blue Dodge Diplomat given to me by my grandfather with hopes of staying indefinitely. When I arrived I introduced myself to the chief and council, who by chance happened to be meeting in the Band Office that day. As it turned out, a journalist they had hired to write a book documenting their efforts to control logging on their traditional lands had arrived the day before. His name was Terry Glavin. They suggested that I see whether he could use any help.

Terry Glavin was on leave from his regular job as a reporter for *Vancouver Sun*. He was kind enough to put up with me, as naive as I was. He knew a few band members and introduced me to them as we proceeded. He was planning to discuss some points of history with William Abraham the next day and invited me to go along. I happily agreed, and so it happened that I encountered William at his camp at Naghatanaqed.

Two cowboys from a nearby cattle ranch had noticed William's camp while searching for strays and had stopped to visit. When we drove up, William and the cowboys were chatting and drinking coffee by a small campfire. His wife Mary was out fishing in a small rowboat. William offered us coffee, pointing to the cups, sugar, and evaporated milk. We prepared our beverages and sat down around the fire to listen to the discussion. The cowboys swapped stories with William for an hour or so and then resumed their eternal quest for strays.

When they left, William turned his attention to Glavin and me. Glavin asked him about several accounts he had mentioned on past occasions. As he had been doing with the cowboys, William spoke in English for our benefit. I sat quietly drinking coffee, absorbing as much of the talk as I could. Hearing that I intended to stay in the valley and study the language, William eventually turned to me and warned me about Tsil'os (Mount Tatlow). Tsil'os, he explained, had been a very difficult man and had been banished by the Chilcotin people. With his wife and children he wandered around the surrounding country until he turned to stone. William looked out at his wife and then nodded in the direction of the highest mountain in the area, a massive formation towering over the lake. Do not point at Tsil'os or do anything else that might offend him, William warned. He delivered this advice matter-of-factly, in the same way that one might give a warning about the perils of a new neighborhood: Be careful. We sat quietly for a time drinking coffee and watching to see whether Mary was catching any fish.

William then began another story. Long ago a white rancher from Chilko Ranch, near what is now Lee's Corner, a small settlement roughly eighty miles to the east, resolved to bring his cattle into Nemiah Valley. William's father-in-law Sam Bulyan warned him that Tsil'os would not look kindly on this, but the man disregarded the warning. Because no one was running cattle in the valley at the time, the grass was lush in the valley. In springtime the man herded his cattle in.

I realized as I listened that the cattle would have come into the valley pretty much where we were sitting, wandering through more or less the way those elusive strays were at that very moment. William continued. In spring and summer the cattle ate well and became fat beyond expectations. It appeared that the rancher would make a great profit. Then, in late summer, a terrible snowstorm hit. It snowed until the cattle were stranded high on a hillside. And still snow continued to fall. Suddenly an avalanche broke away and carried the cattle down the mountain. Almost all of them were crushed. Very few survived, and the man lost a great deal of money. He never tried this again.

After noting the name of the individual involved, William paused to let the story sink in. I wondered about what William intended by the account. Was it nothing more than confirmation of the role Tsil'os plays in the area, or did it speak to the present? Was it a warning for those who were trying to log the area? Was it a warning for Terry and me? Was it a warning for me and other anthropologists who might want to study the Chilcotin language and culture? Or was it perhaps directed at a broader set of historical circumstances that outsiders like Terry and me happened into with the help of the best of intentions and an overabundance of naiveté?

In time, as I was getting to know people at gathering after gathering, I heard the same story many times from many different people. I also noticed that this story and others like it, which also feature the activities of powerful and naive white people, were presented to visitors of all descriptions, whether white or Native, old or young, upon their entry to the valley. Such accounts were presented as this one had been, at gatherings of one kind or another, informally but with purpose.

Historical Narratives and Historical Practice

The study of the folklore of the Pacific Northwest has been dominated by several generations of Boasians. For Franz Boas and his students, myths seem to have played very much the kind of exemplary role in the interpretation of folklore that language played in the interpretation of culture. Boas believed that grammatical categories in particular have the ability to "move along in history more independently of secondary overlays than any other phenomenon of social life" (Silverstein 1979:195). Hence, grammatical categories were given a special role in the reconstruction of culture history. They provided a relatively direct route to the past. Myths were accorded a parallel role in the study of folklore. It was assumed that they have the ability to move along in history more freely than other genres. Thus, priority was given to research on myths, and priority was given to the study of those aspects of myth structure that seem to travel well through time (Boas 1894, 1901, 1902, 1916). In a sense these priorities have traveled through time all too well (Hymes 1981; Jacobs 1959; Sapir 1909).

This is not to say that historical tales or historical narratives were entirely ignored. Boas and his students collected historical narratives as sources of information on the personal lives of informants and translators and as sources of information on the social and cultural changes in process at the time the collections were being made. Nevertheless, in both cases it was understood that the primary purpose of documenting historical narratives was to control the interpretation of myths. Historical narratives were not subject to consideration in their own terms.

The two best known folkloric approaches of today—structural myth analysis and ethnopoetics—developed out of that very Boasian anthropology. Arguably, Claude Lévi-Strauss's most successful structural analysis of a myth, "The Story of Asdiwal" (1968), was conducted on the basis of materials collected by Franz Boas and George Hunt among the Tsimshian at the turn of the century (Boas 1902, 1916; Boas and Hunt 1912). Dell Hymes's pioneering work in ethnopoetics (some of which is collected in Hymes 1981) too was based in significant measure on materials collected by Boas and his students Edward Sapir and Melville Jacobs (Boas 1894; Jacobs 1959; Sapir 1909). Both Lévi-Strauss and Hymes also happened to come directly under the influence of Boas or his students at formative moments in their lives. While structuralism and ethnopoetics have perhaps done more to open the richness of the folklore of Indians of the Pacific Northwest than all other approaches combined, for better or worse they follow the Boasian impetus in emphasizing those aspects of mythical structure that travel through time. The patterns of greatest interest are those that transcend history.

The underlying assumptions of structuralism and ethnopoetics have not gone without criticism. Some have questioned whether these approaches are suited to the multimodal, reflexive, and highly situational techniques by which narratives seem to have been adapted to life in the reservation period (see, e.g., Moore 1993, in press). Roughly thirty years ago Ruth Finnegan observed that collections of folklore had long emphasized text over context, notwithstanding the obvious fact that "the first and most basic characteristic of oral literature . . . is the significance of the actual performance" (1970:2). As Finnegan has explained:

> Oral literature is by definition dependent on a performer who formulates it in words on a specific occasion—there is no other way in which it can be realized as a literary product. In the case of written literature a literary work can be said to have an independent and tangible existence in even one copy, so that questions about, say, the format, number, and publicizing of other written copies can, though not irrelevant, be treated to some extent as secondary; there is, that is, a distinction between the actual creation of a written literary form and its further transmission. The case of oral literature is different. There the connection between transmission and very existence is a much more intimate one, and questions about the means of actual communication are of the first importance—without its oral realization and direct rendition by singer or speaker, an unwritten literary piece cannot easily be said to have any continued or independent existence at all. In this

*respect the parallel is less to written literature than to music and
dance; for these too are art forms which in the last analysis are
actualized in and through their performance and, furthermore, in
a sense depend on repeated performances for their continued exis-
tence. (1970:2)*

In line with Finnegan's insight, other students of contemporary folklore
began to move away from the emphasis on transcendent structures and shift
their analyses toward the problematics of performance.

A performance-oriented approach has obvious advantages over structural analysis and ethnopoetics for the analysis of historical narrative practice, but nevertheless it is important to note that before it can be applied
effectively, more needs to be said about what constitutes performance. The
nature of performance, after all, varies considerably from one art form to
another. When we think of performance in the case of music and dance, we
think immediately of the rapport between performers and audience members. Narrative, in particular, departs from music and dance in that the
relationship between performer and audience is resituated, or embedded,
within the interplay between narrative and narrating scenarios. Recent work
on oral and written literature suggests, indeed, that much of the power of
literature resides precisely in its capacity for activating the "there-and-then"
in the "here-and-now" (Bauman 1986; Gennette 1980; Onega and Landa
1996; Parmentier 1993; Silverstein 1999). This work suggests not only that
performance is emergent in oral narrative (Hymes 1981:81) but that the
parameters of the performance event—including even the identities of performers and audience members—can be derived from narrative scenarios.

Thus, whereas it is undeniably true that "performance" is intrinsic to oral
narrative, the activities of performers and audience members can only be
approached in the most superficial terms without reference to the narrative
scenarios being activated in the performance event. For this reason some
have argued that performance and text both are best understood as unfolding within an encompassing social-textual process called entextualization/
contextualization (Bauman and Briggs 1990; Silverstein and Urban 1996).

This third approach is best suited to historical narratives. It captures the
strengths of both text-oriented and performance-oriented approaches. It
addresses the social properties of narrative and the textual properties of
performance. The engine of the entextualizing process is the social organization of the relations between the elements of two different realms of activity,
the narrated and the narrating. Roman Jakobson (1971) used the term *narrative event* to designate the goings-on recounted in narrative. Narrated events
have properties of their own. Some conform to our experience of reality in

the everyday world; some do not. Some are set far away and long ago; some are closer to home in space and time. Narrative types can be identified on the basis of the properties of narrative events. Thus, sometimes tales are identified by the presence of supernatural elements in narrative events.

Narrative events tend to center on the activities of persons or person-like beings. Following Melville Jacobs (1959), I will refer to the central players in the narrated events as actors or narrative actors. Some actors conform to our experience of actual persons; some do not. The characteristics of actors also can be used to identify types of narrative, as when myths are identified on the basis of the presence of other than human actors. The organization of the portrayal of relations among narrative actors in narrative events is a vitally important dimension of narrative practice. Some narratives emphasize the point of view of one narrative actor throughout; some emphasize the points of view of different narrative actors at different points in the narrative.

A consideration of narrative would be incomplete without taking into account the events in which narratives are recounted. Following Jakobson again, I will term these narrating events. Narrating events occur in culturally and spatiotemporally specific settings. The properties of narrating events can be subject to anthropological scrutiny. Though it is perhaps less common, it is no less practical to classify narratives on the basis of the properties of narrating events than it is to do so on the basis of the properties of narrated events.

Every narrative has a narrator, or narrators, and a "narratee," or narratees, and some have in addition an audience. Those parties have statuses in the here and now that must be analytically distinguished from the statuses of those they portray in the narrative events, even if they happen to be portraying themselves, their interlocutors, or their audience in past actions. Thus, in sum, I am distinguishing two kinds of events: narrated and narrating events. On the basis of this distinction, I am further distinguishing between two kinds of participants: narrative actors and actors in the speech event of narration. While the distinctions between narrative and narrated events correspond more or less to the everyday concepts of narrative, on the one hand, and performance setting, on the other, my intent in establishing them is not to reinforce the differences between the two as these are generally understood but, rather, to open for systemic inquiry the interactions between them.

Public Events: The Setting

Intuition suggests that in the case of Chilcotin historical narrative there is a meaningful relationship between narrated and narrating events. The content of the narratives seems to bear in some way on the nature of the situations in which they are delivered. The narrative events center on actors who may be white or Chilcotin. They feature actions that epitomize either violations of or appropriate expressions of Chilcotin values. The accounts are presented at public events attended by many outsiders—some who are relatives and friends who for the moment assume the interests of the local group and others, who may or may not be relatives, who assume the interests of the local group while pursuing agendas of their own.

Occasionally in these situations the question of group membership is addressed directly. Particularly after a drink to two, one party might inquire directly of another, "Who are you? Where do you come from?" When such inquiries were made to me, friends would intercede to explain that I was living in the valley with them or that I was learning to speak the language. Then they generally asked if I was a missionary, and the matter was left at that. For the most part, however, such questions are felt but left unaddressed. What is in question in such events, however, is not merely whether a particular person has genealogical ties to the group or whether another is known to be friendly. What is at issue is where people stand in relation to the ultimate principal, or entity responsible, for the event. And the question of the principal of the event is complicated by the fact that virtually all "public" events on the reserve are presided over by outsiders. Marriages and funerals are presided over by priests. Band meetings are presided over by the chief and counsel. Chief and counsel are officials of the federal government, whatever else they are, and whether at any particular moment they are acting in their capacity as local representatives or in their capacity as government employees is very much on the minds of band members. The rodeo is organized by the local rodeo club, but the event is sponsored by a regional rodeo association. The emcee represents the rodeo association. In a very real sense, then, the officials who preside over public events are based in the outside world.

All of these events exhibit a pattern of dual organization. The events are planned and prepared by local community members. At a certain point outside dignitaries arrive. On cue they move to the center of the activity where they play their part. Local community members who to that point are involved in preparations, or perhaps their own affairs, aggregate in a ring around the activity. Thus, a second activity group coalesces around the primary one. Most local community members find themselves in this secondary group, shoulder to shoulder with those who have come in to observe. As the events come to a close, the primary activity ceases, and all the outside personages leave the valley, often very quickly. Life resumes, with perhaps an intensification of solidarity on the basis of a renewed sense of sharing a place (see Silverstein 1998:403–406).

Hugh Brody's description of a funeral among the Beaver Indians (Athabaskan speakers) of the Fort Nelson area of northern British Columbia illustrates the pattern well. The atmosphere was jovial on the day of the funeral. The people engaged in preparation seemed to be enjoying each others' company. Brody himself pitched in and eventually accompanied a small group to the church:

> *Windswept and laughing, we arrived at the hall. Outside some children were playing, and a small group of men and women stood talking. Buddy and I went in and found the service under way. A young priest, robed and looking hopelessly uncomfortable, stood in front of two batches of chairs. He was reading a passage about Jesus being love. He showed signs of great nervousness. His voice was urgent and exaggeratedly mellifluous, as if he were trying to force his way through much tangible resistance. Yet there were very few people in the seats: three visitors from town, the Reserve's teachers, the Chief (a young woman at that time occupied this elected position) with three or four elders, and two women. The elders and women were very upset and crying loudly, murmuring words I could not understand, and leaning on, almost clutching the Chief who was sitting between them. A man lay on the floor at the back of the church, behind the chairs. He was unconscious, presumably from drink. The elders and the two crying women kept getting up from their seats. Twice they walked to the coffin, leaned against it, and called out loudly in a painful show of unhappiness. At the same time, children were coming and going from the hall to the entrance of the church, talking noisily to one another.*
>
> *Buddy and I stood at the doorway to the church for a while. The priest persisted, acknowledging all the disturbance only in the tone of his voice. When he had said some prayers, one of the schoolteachers began to read a long passage from the Bible. The shouts and footfalls of children now playing tag in the main part of the hall added to the noise. The man lying at the back did not stir. The service just carried on, the priest and teachers doing it their way, while the Indians did it theirs. (1988:76–79)*

In the Chilcotin equivalents, which I witnessed on many occasions, the church on such occasions would be surrounded with vehicles and people, monitoring the service from a distance while communing with one another.

The communication that takes place at the center of such gatherings is in a sense always indirect. In the funeral Brody describes, the priest's words are not meant to represent his feelings but the word of the Gospel. And while Brody's account suggests that it makes little difference whether the priest's words are heard or understood by those assembled, at Nemiah Valley, where funeral services are almost identical, it matters very much that the priest delivers his lines. Even if he is not considered an authority in all areas of life, he is considered the authority on such occasions. His part is crucial to the appropriate execution of weddings, funerals, and many other events.

Other visitors, too, are greatly appreciated, insofar as they do not over-estimate their role. For example, I was once asked to participate in a wedding of a good friend. I was concerned about what was entailed, imagining being expected to add a personal dimension to the ceremony in the style of the weddings of my colleagues in graduate school (1980s Chicago). I was in-formed that my part in the Chilcotin wedding was to read faithfully a preselected passage. The passage testified to the author's love of Christ. While the passage was obviously composed for a practicing Catholic, my inviters knew well that I was not. That fact did not, it turned out, preclude a meaningful reading. After the ceremony, the priest, who also knew I was not Catholic, thanked me and explained that it is often difficult to find people willing to read in weddings. In spite of the incongruity of the situation from my point of view, my effort was apparently appreciated, as I later discovered when a picture of me reading earnestly was included among many others to mark the occasion in a photo album of the wedding formally given to the bride several months after the wedding. I was pleased that I had not embar-rassed my friend.

The communicative dynamic of such public events is epitomized in the act of reading. Whether church service or band meeting, the central focus of such events is almost always the reading of documents, the taking of notes, or both. The paper scripting of such performances enhances the sense that officials are not acting on their own behalf; they are performing specific parts on behalf of others (see McLaughlin 1992). Like the priest, and like me at the wedding, they cannot and routinely do not assume that they are acting on their own behalf. To borrow Erving Goffman's terminology for charac-terizing kinds of communicative footing (1981), central actors in such events serve as *animators* of others' positions. When they compose what they say, they serve as *authors*. But in carrying out their official duties, they are careful not to suggest that they are personally acting as the *principals*. Communica-tion emanating from officials at the center of public events characteristically avoids reference to personal interest, or local family interest, and in this sense is always indirect.

The communication that takes place in the outer circle of public events might easily be seen as functionally peripheral. However, it is important to see that the people in the outer circle come very close to embodying the principal, in Goffman's sense, for the entire event. Insofar as they see themselves as Indians "from around here," inhabitants of the outer circle are what the event as a whole is really about. The question, however, is how they see themselves. Given that historical narratives are the prevailing form of communication here, it is not unreasonable to assume that they bear scrutiny for what they reveal about the process of self-reflection and self-identification as conducted in the outer circle. Maurice Halbwachs's observations on the localization of memories are pertinent here: "What makes recent memories hang together is not that they are contiguous in time: it is rather that they are part of a totality of thoughts common to a group, the group of people with whom we have a relation at this moment, or with whom we have had a relation on the preceding day or days. To recall them it is hence sufficient that we place ourselves in the perspective of this group, that we adopt its interests and follow the slant of its reflections" (1992:52).

Recording the "Text"

Developing an analytic perspective on the relations between narrated and narrating events in the unfolding of text requires attention to the details of performance. I did not, however, record the narrative that William Abraham presented to me upon my arrival in the valley. Frankly, for a time I put narratives like the one William presented to me out of my mind. They were so commonplace that I began to overlook them. Only belatedly did I begin to sense their importance. Then I resolved to tape-record the narrative of the man who brought in the first herd of cattle. By that time four or five months had past, and I had been swept into daily life at Nemiah Valley. The band had kindly put me up in a reserve house, along with a man named Daniel Abraham (one of William's many sons). Daniel was recently divorced. He was out of a house and looking for work. He had been an instructor in the Chilcotin language some years back, and I offered to pay him to help me study the language. I paid him when we were working formally and otherwise kept a place in the house by buying propane and groceries.

People often stopped by in the morning looking for a ride to town. If I drove them to town, someone else would appear when I returned, also looking for a ride or looking for a warm body to help drag a dead moose out of the woods. Others stopped by looking for someone to help cut up fresh salmon, even out teams for playing horseshoes, or serve as audience for impromptu performances of country music.

While I enjoyed all of these activities, I was in highest demand as what one community member labeled a "taxi driver." My neighbors Erving Richard and his wife Charmagne Bouchant and child Conrad, to the east, and his brother Johnny Richard and his wife Lucile, to the south, enjoyed traveling back and forth to town, and as they were elderly, they enjoyed very much having a driver. Between the two families, I was occupied driving one or the other on most weekends and at many other times as well. Given that a trip to town (Williams Lake) takes three hours one way, this obviously involves a good deal of time.

In some ways being a taxi driver was as convenient for me as it was for the riders. Erving or Johnny would sit next to me and tell me about the places we passed along the way. I could participate in conversations in both English and Chilcotin (with the men speaking in English and Chilcotin and the women speaking almost exclusively in Chilcotin). For Johnny Richard, in particular, the a trip to town was generally punctuated on the return trip by the consumption of such delicacies as smoked baby oysters washed down with sips from pint-sized bottles of fortified wine. He and Lucile would shift to the back seat, intermittently leaning forward from their reclined position to feed me an oyster.

One Sunday morning when Johnny stepped into the house, however, I was less than enthused at the prospect of driving to town. Though we had discussed sitting down to talk about the Chilcotin language more formally, I was so busy driving that I never had an opportunity to record either Johnny or Francis at their homes. I had chosen not to press my interests and on numerous occasions had passed on opportunities to record narratives when they were presented. Indeed, I was informed by one community leader that to her surprise the elders seemed to enjoy my presence, especially the fact that I was not always asking for something, a form of behavior they associated with anthropologists. When Johnny asked whether I would drive him and his wife to town that morning, however, the impatient anthropologist in me emerged as I imagined another lengthy drive and several days in town trying to locate people. So I told him, fine, I would do it, but I would dearly appreciate it if he would first sit down with me and tell his account of Spencer, the man who first herded cattle into Nemiah Valley, in the Chilcotin language, so that I could tape-record it. He agreed without hesitation for reasons I will never be sure of, given the way I handled the situation. Was he ready to present the account all along, or did he simply want to get to town? I will never know. If I acted impertinently, he chose not to acknowledge that fact and presented his account in his usual pleasant demeanor.

He sat down at our kitchen table. I set up the microphone and turned on the tape recorder. He then turned to me to see whether I was ready, and seeing that I was, he began. He narrated his account at a steady and unhurried pace. It took about twenty minutes. Just as he finished I realized that I had not in fact pushed the record button on the tape recorder. This did not seem to surprise Johnny, who by that point in my stay knew very well that on certain select occasions I failed to achieve even a modicum of practical competence. I fixed the machine and asked whether he would mind presenting his account again, thinking to myself that I had probably just missed an opportunity. He agreed without hesitation again and narrated the account exactly, to my ear, the same way he had the first time. This time the tape recorder worked.

Obviously, these were not the ideal conditions for recording an authentic version of an oral narrative, but there were nonetheless some indications that Johnny presented his account much as he usually did. First of all, he embellished the account I asked for with another. He used the latter to frame the former in a very interesting way. Second, Daniel Abraham, who was also present during this entire episode, quietly intruded with "That's it," which is in fact audible on the recorded tape, just as Johnny wrapped up. Based on prior hearings Daniel knew well where the account ended, and his past hearings served him well. Third, awkward as it was, the situation was not entirely different in character from those in which this sort of narrative is typically delivered. Not that they are generally presented for tape recording by taxi-driver-wannabe-anthropologists, but, as seen above, they are typically delivered on the fly, as it were, in situations in which the audience is not expected to control all the protocols that might be expected of insiders to the tradition.

The recording was made on 4 September 1991. I have arranged a transcript of the account in a variant of a format developed by Robert Moore (1993). Moore uses columns to indicate Jakobson's speech event modalities: stretches of discourse situated in the narrating speech event are set on the left margin; stretches of discourse set within the narrated events are indented two steps to the right. I have further highlighted the difference through the use of *italics* for discourse situated in the narrating event and **bold roman** for discourse situated in the narrated events. What are found on the left, then, are Johnny's comments directed at me, mine to him, and his interpretive framing of the narrative. To the right are the narrative line and speech acts set within the narrative line. For convenience I have titled the transcript "Spencer":

Spencer

David Dinwoodie: *Spencer. . . .*
Johnny Richard: *Start over again?*
DD: *Uh huh.*
JR: *Yeah.* [2 sec]
I(i)

ʔéspénses jíyílhníh,
'Spencer, they said to him,'
jíyuzish,
'they called him,'
nenqayní . . . gwedúwh.
'Indian people around here.'
Yagh Chílko Ránch bets'enz haghint'i. [6 sec]
'Chilko Ranch was his property.'
II(i)

Yagh, ʔéstórekéeper hát'in haghint'i. [2 sec]
'He had a storekeeper.'
10   *ʔeyen . . .* [5 sec]
'That one [Spencer],'
yeʔad húnt'ín saghint'i [3 sec]
'he [Spencer] must have liked his [the storekeeper's] wife.'
(ii)

Gúyen stórekeeper ʔeyen
'That one [the storekeeper]'
máil tsinsh . . . ʔánálí ʔan. [3 sec]
'handled the mail too.'
          Yagh yédéstl'és hanlhtsana . . . ʔéyi,
          'So he [the storekeeper] found his [Spencer's] letter,'
15   *gan gu stránge gant'ih*
'but it was strange.'
Yagh,
'Uhm,'
          "strange letter . . . ʔan náhústén"
          ' "Strange letter . . . I'll investigate," '
          yenizen.
          'he [the storekeeper] thought.'
ʔéyi déstl'és ʔéyi yedetázganz,
'He opened that letter,'
20   *gúyen stórekéeper,* [5 sec]
'the storekeeper,'

(iii)

    hink'an . . . gúyen ʔéspénces,
    'and . . . that Spencer,'
    yádéh ʔilhch'és táh ʔégun,
    'somewhere far in the east,'
    ʔilhútáh ʔajágh,
    'he did something,'

25   *seníya lhan desanh,*
    'probably for lots of money,'
    qa deni ch'adínlágh desaghint'i.
    'he must have killed a person.'
    ʔilhutáh ʔajágh.
    'He did something like that.'
    ʔéyed guyen stórekéeper, jégughintan.   [3 sec]
    'That storekeeper, he had found out.'
        ʔéspénces ʔegwiyénízín
        'Spencer realized'

30   bedéstl'és dedets'exízganz.   [3 sec]
        'his letter had been opened.'

(iv)

        ʔuh . . . Stórekéeper ʔéyen . . .
        'Uh . . . the storekeeper [and another] . . .'
        gugun . . . Dábéy Allén ts'egwedish ʔegun   [3 sec]
        'to the place called Davey Allen,'
        ʔegun náh nájádílh ʔan.   [2 sec]
        'they went there.'
    Yagh midugh ʔéyun belh sághint'í.   [3 sec]
    'Must have been another white man with him.'

(v)

35   Yagh ʔéspénces . . . shótgún hinlhchúd   [3 sec]
        'Spencer . . . grabbed a shotgun.'
        "Hútághálnílhʔ"
        ' "What are you going to do?" '
        jiyelhnihanh.
        'they asked him.'
        "Dish qa yétásdálh ʔan,"
        ' "I will hunt for spruce grouse," '
        "ʔelhtílh desanh."
        ' "ruffed grouse [those in groups in trees] maybe." '

40   ʔeyen . . . gwech'énilhqíz yax Dábéy Allén.
'That one [Spencer] drove away toward Davey
Allen.'

ʔánilhqíz
'When he drove up,'
gúyen . . . midugh . . . stórekéeper desaghint'i ʔeyed
'it must have been that white storekeeper,'
yedéstl'és . . . naghilh'ín ʔéyen.   [4 sec]
'the one who saw his [Spencer's] letter.'

        Yadenílh[telh] . . .
        'He [Spencer] shot . . .'

45   Ga . . . naqayélhtsín desaghint'i.   [2 sec]
'he [Spencer] must have wounded him [the
storekeeper].'

Sanqí. . . .
'Difficult. . . .'

        "Chayedinlagh,"
        ' "I killed him," '
        yenizen.
        'he [Spencer] thought.'

Tatílhts'éd saghint'i.   [2 sec]
'It [made him] run, must have.'

50   *ʔéspénces . . . nílhjúd desaghint'i.*
'Spencer must have been scared.'
The . . . her name's Nátídál.
'The . . . the name of the place is He-did-not-leave.'

        Yaz gunés tílhgáy . . .
        'He walked south . . .'
        uhm . . . táxédélt'í . . .   [4 sec]
        'and dove in . . .'
        ʔegun . . . lha gunán nabíl   [2 sec]
        'he did not swim across there [i.e., make it],'

55   tughezílhghín.   [2 sec]
        'he drowned.'

(vi)

ʔegun . . . beqá ts'énutáh ts'édísh.   [3 sec]
'Then . . . they searched for him, they say.'
Gu dení lhan nenqayní,
'There were many Indian people,'
Anaham deni saghit'i,
'Anaham people probably,'

jiqanátah
'they were looking for him'
60 *guguwh . . . tabanx . . . river tabanx.*
'in the area of the river banks.'
ʾegúh . . .
'Pretty soon . . .'
Gúyen Jélí,
'that one Jerry,'
jiyalhághínih
'they called him'
"Jeli . . ."
' "Jerry . . ." '
65 *jedih ʾéyen.*   [3 sec]
'is what they call him.'
(vii)

Díamond ríng saghint'i,
'Must have been a diamond ring,'
ke . . . belá tuhághálʾah . . . qa.
'that [ring], his hand extending out of the water,'
bech'ed ʾasa díndín
'on it the sun sparkled,'
bech'ed ʾasa detlig,
'on it the sun shone,'
70 *diamond ring,*
'the diamond ring,'
ʾegúh . . . jíyinlhtín ʾan.   [7 sec]
'when he [Jerry] found him [Spencer].'
(viii)

Yagh gwentsén jíyénáxánéntist'ín, desaghint'i.
'He experienced something awful, must have.'
Gwech'ez . . . gúyen yagulnig hagwézlíd ʾeyen
'Because . . . he was afraid that that one [the storekeeper]
would report him,'
yadenulhtelh qấʾát'in.
'he [Spencer] tried to shoot him [the storekeeper].'
75 *Guyen yedestl'és yedetázgánz,*   [4 sec]
'The one [the storekeeper] that opened his [Spencer's] letter,'
ʾegúh ʾéspénces lha gul,
'Spencer is gone,'

ch'adéjágh saghint'i
'he must have died,'
drowned selin.
'become drowned.'
lha jid gunán naghubigúyah
'He couldn't swim across to the other side,'
80   *tuyezílhxín.*   [7 sec]
'the water overwhelmed him.'

III(i)

ʔeyen desaghint'i,
'It must have been him,'
nendúwh lha ched deni gúl . . .
'not many people around here,'
gúlísh sagughint'í nenduwh
'must have been very few around here,'
lha gwechah nulh,
'not many animals,'
85   *lha gwechah nazlhiny*
'not many horses.'
Nazlhiny dzáh sú gúlín desaghint'i.
'Must have been only horses.'
Tl'ugh dináz,
'The grass was tall,'
nendúwh gádádinlh naz
'it was this tall,'
two, three foot
'two, three foot,'
90   *just oh, two-and-a-half-foot-, two-, three-foot-long tl'ugh.*
'just oh, two-and-a-half-foot-, two-, three-foot-long grass.'
ʔegúh . . . nenqayní chéh
'and in Chilcotin'
deni qi tay, nanqi ts'edah, heh heh.
'three, two human feet it is called, heh heh.'
             ʔegúh [2 sec] **Nendúwh ní néníyúd xi di ghilí.**
             'He [Spencer] herded them [his cattle] to this area
             after the winter.'

(ii)

             ʔabá ghilí:
             'My late father:'

95   "ʔéyed Tsil'os, bígwení . . .
     ' "that [inanimate] Tsil'os, he'll frighten you . . .'
     "bígweníjed hánt'áh,
     ' "he'll frighten you for certain,'
     "xedaxuntan!"
     ' "Watch yourself!" '
     yenáhán.
     'he told him.'
     Sám Richard ts'edah haghint'i,
     'He was called Sam Richard,'

100   *seʔábá ghili . . . ʔíyen.*   [4 sec]
     'my late father, that one.'

(iii)

     ʔegúh qi . . . deni qí diny,
     'Then . . . four human feet,'
     nendúwh dení t'iz . . . gwedúwh gadinlhchugh
     'here, above a person's sternum . . . that deep'
     naghajéz.   [3 sec]
     'it snowed.'
     Guh xidi guh . . . ʔegú sek'í tl'ugh xiyán.
     'All winter . . . the cows ate grass.'

105   ʔaghúlhts'én . . . ʔaghúlhts'én gwédénzil.
     'in spring . . . it became warm.'
     Yagh yes naxísdan,
     'The snow began shifting,'
     yes detli selín.
     'the snow became soft.'
     Yáduwh gwenén sek'í nálhʔás
     'When the cows were grazing far up on the side,'
     ʔéyi lhan nálhʔás,
     'many cows were grazing,'

110   ʔéyi xedax
     'they [cows] slid [in an avalanche],'
     xedax.
     'they slid.'
     bezék'í belh gwédax, bezék'í,
     'his cows slid with the avalanche, his cows,'
     gan ʔegúh . . . ʔelh . . . bélh jídágwendi yatsunsh.
     'and then . . . together . . . they slid down with it.'
     Gatsi hilín sélín,
     'It happened to almost all of them,'

115   *seven hundred desaghint'i,*   [7 sec]
'it must have been seven hundred,'
ʔilhed ch'ilhghilganílt'í hándéd desaghínt'i,
'seven hundred it must have been,'
k'es ʔelhchántey hándéd desaghínt'i.
'or six hundred, it must have been.'
ʔéyi, gats'í hílín sélín,
'Those, it happened to almost all of them,'
      tad *ʔelhch'anághan guʔan ʔesgulá dzá*
      'only thirty-five'

120   **gúdéh gújénaghiyud . . . ʔegúh.**   [8 sec]
      'he herded back east.'

(iv)

ʔegúh, lha gwech'íz gudéz sek'í xénáníyélh.
'Then, he never brought cows from the east again.'
ʔegúh, nengwédzá gájágh,
'That is all he did,'
lha nendín xénágúlal
'he did not return this way.'

(v)

      Nendín néngúshúd
      'I'm going to land grab here.'

125   **yenizen.**
      'he thought.'
ʔeguh lha j . . . heh heh,
'but no . . . heh heh,'
lha jid gaghunax guyal,
'he couldn't do that at all,'
gwechugh . . . nén . . .
'much . . . land . . .'
Tsil'os yets'én néntsén, aheh aheh.
'Tsil'os spoiled it for him, aheh aheh.'
nén gwegúwh dzá sagunt'i.
'That must be all for that.'

Daniel Abraham: *That's it.*

Johnny Richard's account of Spencer bringing cattle to the valley includes the main points of all the other accounts I heard of that set of events, including William Abraham's. This is perhaps not surprising given the fact that Johnny and William are brothers-in-law. Sam Richard was head of the dominant family in the valley at one time. William came out from Toosey

Reserve when he was a young man, more or less apprenticed himself to Sam, and married Sam's daughter Marie. Johnny, along with Erving, is one of the middle sons. Marie is Johnny's older sister. Consequently, Sam Richard is a major figure for both William and Johnny, as he is for many other residents of the valley, and is obviously the ultimate source of the account (though, given the wide circulation of these stories, not necessarily the immediate source). Johnny's account, however, differs from all other accounts of Spencer that I had heard in that he prefaced it with Spencer's ultimate demise.

The account shares basic features of content with many other historical narratives. In all, men pursue activities that lead toward their demise. The activities are generally those connected to ranching, cattle, crops, or ranch business. The featured actors are generally white ranchers, though many variations are evident whereby Chilcotin Indians act like white ranchers or white ranchers act uncharacteristically like Chilcotin Indians. The ranching era has begun to give way to the reserve era of Department of Indian Affairs contracts, tourism, logging, and to some extent mining. But ranching continues on a modest scale, and one senses that these stories have continuing application to a qualified tradition. These accounts are all set in a time not long before the present. In one sense that era has passed; in another sense it is very much still alive: genealogical ties to actors are still active, the places featured in these accounts are still known, and the broader interethnic situation has only intensified.

Two more brief examples highlight the commonalities of various instances of the genre. I recorded one example from a man who was not the original "author" but who had been part of the intended audience (as I was too, in this case) of the first telling. Jack English, a Chilcotin man from Anaham Reserve, was visiting William Abraham at his cabin at Naghbas one night, during a later portion of the same journey mentioned at the opening of this chapter. Jack was in the area working on a fencing contract and was looking for company. Again I was present with Terry Glavin. Jack presented an account of a man who was stealing cattle. His habit attracted the attention of the devil himself. I did not record the account at the time. Months later when visiting William at his home in Nemiah Valley I asked if he would mind retelling what Jack had presented. He summarized in English as follows:

> He [Jack] said that other fella, you know, he, gonna go outside toilet. That fella you know, he steals cattle all the time. Pretty soon that Lejab [the Devil] starting bothering him. So this, this fella he go, nighttime, I guess, he go outside in the toilet. So that Lejab— sitting in the toilet I guess—and that Lejab started talk to him.

First he say, "We going to give you lots of money [if] you keep going like that. We'll be your friend." So he got scared. He used to stay way up Indian meadow up on top in Alexis Creek. That's where he used to stay and steal somebody's cattle, them calves and stuff like that. Pretty soon he seen Nentsen [Evil]. Nentsen started talked to him, and he say, "You keep going like that, we'll give you lots of money. Give you so much you can't run out any money no more."

So he got scared, and then he took off down, down Anaham. So he started stay there, and then he don't wanna go back no more. I guess Nentsen scared the hell out of him, heh heh!

William finished by giving the identity of the man in question and telling me where he lived, noting that he was still alive at that time. In this account the man desists in his behavior once it becomes clear to him that it is characteristically white.

Another example features a white cowboy-rancher. William presented this account to me when I asked about a new road sign bearing the name Robertson's Crossing. I did not have a tape recorder with me at the time, but later I returned to his house and asked whether he would mind recording it. A summary of the translation of the recorded account runs as follows:

Robertson was related to the Indian Johnny Setah. Robertson had land at the other end of the valley (Xeni, or Nemiah Valley). One time Johnny Setah went to see him. He found Robertson dead on his floor where he had killed himself. The police came, as did Robertson's relatives. They buried him on a hill behind his house and later returned to put up a headstone. Then they put a fence around him. Pretty soon the Chilcotin man Lashuway Lulua bought that land.

What followed is rendered more precisely at it was presented:

ʔeguh hink'an shunchuh
'And at some point,'
guyen nenqayni gadeni
'that Indian talked about it'
ʔeguh Johnny Setah,
'that one Johnny Setah'

Guyen midugh ʔilhes bedaghaganlh.
'That white man is really starving'

5   *Gan yax guneh gwetax gwenilhjez*
      'But over in the bush where he marked out (a garden)'
      ʾegun lhan xenelhyax,
      'he's growing vegetables there,'
      lhan yahadzish.
      'he gave away a great deal.'
      Guyen midugh sek'i tehat'in
      'That white man had cows,'
      ʾilhes ts'engwetegwedits'en
      'he is really not stingy,'
10   *guwh gant'ih k'asel bedagaynsh*
      'that is the way he nearly starved'
      guwh bedaganysh
      'that way he nearly starved'
      gwech'ez xenilch'agh
      'that is why he became mad,'
      gweqa naxadenilhtelh
      'and for that reason he killed himself,'

      saghini denish,
      'he speculated that is probably why,'
15   *Johnny Setah.*
      'Johnny Setah.'

He died because he gave away everything, even to the point of giving away what he needed to survive. His behavior exemplifies, then, the Chilcotin virtue of generosity. Whereas the rustler was Indian by birth and white by comportment, Robertson was white by birth and Chilcotin by comportment. William underscores this when he mentions that Robertson was given a Chilcotin funeral. And Johnny Setah who was there as witness also pretty much says as much. It is perhaps not insignificant that the Robertson story eventually results in the land returning to Chilcotin possession.

Melville Jacobs's observations on a Galice historical event text capture the essence of the genre's themes:

> *Several expressive items are imbedded here. One is the lamentable destiny of a person who ignores warning, even of lethal danger. Throughout the oral literatures of the bands and hamlets of the northwest states, myth actors who, in a regional kind of bull-headedness that verged on suicidal compulsion, were proceeding to their doom were admonished and at once blandly disregarded*

what they heard. I think the region accepted a premise that was at once of a psychological kind about person's autonomous choices, and of a philosophically fatalistic kind. Narrators expressed it frequently in oral genres. It exhibits a conviction that no person can be persuaded, certainly he can never be forced, to halt or protect himself if, in a kind of extremity of individual autonomy that is abetted, even straitjacketed, by his personal supernaturals, he chooses to march into a situation from which withdrawal is impossible. Indians therefore would not think of forcibly halting a person who had advanced in the direction of a denouement that was certain death. Such respect for other persons' choices, such conviction that they could not and would not listen to advice to be cautious, such fatalism from the point of view of Western ideology, are alien to most Euroamericans. Such policy expressed acceptance of a tragic destiny, in a frame of proper northwest states' Indian etiquette, values, and orientation about people's self-identities. They were unchangeably what they were. They did what they did. Their direction was unalterable. Nothing could change such people, such events, such reality. (1968:188–189)

All that remains to be said is that these narratives are delivered in everyday language. They are stylistically informal, and the occasions on which they are delivered are relatively unmarked. Their modest presence seems to have enabled them to flourish as an art and a tradition.

"Walking" through the Text

Here I develop a "reading" of "Spencer" from the point of view of a hypothetical narratee. Johnny Richard begins by introducing a name and, after a brief false start, characterizing the community in which it was used ("Spencer, they said to him, they called him, Indian people around here"). He then introduces a morally loaded attribute (Bauman 1986:60), namely, the fact that "Chilko Ranch was his [Spencer's] property." Located on a rare piece of arable land, the ranch stands to this day—roughly seventy miles east of Nemiah Valley—as a symbol of the separation of Chilcotin peoples from natural resources. Indirectly, Johnny has introduced two communities: Indian people around here and non-Indian people around there. By using the perfect aspect and the name of a ranch of known location (instead of "long ago and far away"), he sets a real and yet finite distance between the events to be described and the present. The distance is reinforced when he does not indicate that he experienced them firsthand, when he might have been expected to do so. On the other hand, the finiteness of the distance, notwithstanding the lack of indication of his own presence, keeps open the possibility that someone who was present composed the original account of these events and relayed it to him or to someone who relayed it to him. In other words, the finiteness of the distance keeps open the possibility that someone specific (a narrator) or something tangible (a narration) links the narrating present and the narrated past.

The story of the linkage, if it were to exist, would be of necessity integral to this historical account. It is through such a linkage that the narratee might learn how the actions of there-and-then bear on the here-and-now. The linkage being implied but not specified results in a dilemma for the narratee: the events being described may well relate to the present, but it remains unclear how. If the implied narrator happened to be a member of one or another of the pertinent communities, that might well be the key.

In this opening section, which is labeled I on the transcript, then, Johnny accomplishes an extraordinary amount of metapragmatic work. He establishes roles in the speech event (narrator, narratee) and fills those roles with himself and yours truly; he establishes roles in the narrated event (actors, others) and fills them with Spencer, on the one hand, and Indians around here, on the other. And he implies that a figure may exist that might mediate between the narrated and narrating events but gives no indications as to how.

What follows this condensed opening is a somewhat extended account of Spencer's demise. Though not the account of central interest, it constitutes a narrative in its own right. This account is labeled II on the transcript. From one point of view it is nothing more than a complicated way of introducing yet another morally loaded attribute of Spencer before getting to the heart of the matter, namely, the dubious circumstances under which he passed away. From another point of view, it is a means for establishing a rhetorical pattern, or poetic rhythm.

The narrative is organized into eight units, each distinguished by an internal emphasis on one actor:

(i)   Spencer

(ii)   Storekeeper

(iii)   Spencer

(iv)   Storekeeper

(v)   Spencer

(vi)   Jerry (Chilcotin man who found Spencer's body)

(vii)   Spencer's Diamond Ring

(viii)   Spencer

Spencer is most prominent in the first three lines (9–11): "He [Spencer] had a storekeeper. That one [Spencer], he [Spencer] must have liked his [the storekeeper's] wife." The storekeeper is most prominent in the following nine lines (12–20): "That one [the storekeeper] handled the mail too. So he [the storekeeper] found his [Spencer's] letter, but it was strange. Uhm, 'strange letter . . . I'll investigate,' he [the storekeeper] thought. He opened that letter, the storekeeper." Spencer returns to front and center in the next ten lines (22–31): "and . . . that Spencer, somewhere far in the east, he did something, probably for lots of money, he must have killed a person. He did something like that. That storekeeper, he had found out. Spencer realized his letter had been opened." The storekeeper returns to front and central in the following four lines: "Uh, the storekeeper [and another] . . . to the place called Davey Allen, they went there. Must have been another white man with him." Then the focus returns to Spencer for what appears to be the climax:

> Spencer . . . grabbed a shotgun. "What are you going to do," they asked him? "I will hunt for spruce grouse, ruffed grouse maybe" [he said]. That one [Spencer] drove away toward Davey Allen. When he drove up, it must have been that white storekeeper, the one who saw his [Spencer's] letter. He [Spencer] shot . . . he [Spencer] must have wounded him [the storekeeper]. Difficult. . . . "I killed him," he [Spencer] thought. It [made him] run, must have. Spencer must have been scared. The name of the place is He-did-not-leave. He walked south . . . and dove in . . . he did not swim across there, he drowned.

At this point a wrinkle is introduced into the pattern. The section spanning the next ten lines (56–65) focuses not on the actions of Spencer or the storekeeper but on the actions of local Indians and on the actions of a man named Jerry in particular: "They searched for him, they say. There were many Indian people, Anaham people probably, they were looking for him in the area of the river banks. Pretty soon . . . that one Jerry, they called him Jerry . . . is what they call him." Next follows a section that comes back to Spencer in a way. It is about another morally loaded attribute of Spencer's— the fact that he wore a diamond ring and the fact that the diamond ring gave him away: "Must have been a diamond ring, that [ring], his hand extending out of the water, on it the sun sparkled, on it the sun shone, the diamond ring, when he [Jerry] found him." Finally, the narrative is summarized in a way that emphasizes the fact that Spencer is dead for certain.

Shifts in narrative focus are signaled in nearly every section of part II by the use of the demonstrative *guyen* 'that,' together with a proper name (e.g.,

Spencer) or a definite description (e.g., the storekeeper), and by changing the grammatical subject. A closer look shows that other grammatical resources are used to underscore actor focus within discourse segments. For example, where there might be some doubt as to which actor is primary, the definite article ʔ*eyen* 'the [human]' is used to signal continuity of actor focus, as in lines 9–11, "He[i] had a storekeeper[j]. (ʔ*eyen*[i]) That one[i], he[i] must have liked his[j] wife."

Another linguistic element utilized in underscoring continuity of actor focus is evident in line 11 of section II(i), *yeʔad húntʼín saghintʼi* 'he must have liked the storekeeper's wife.' *Ye-* 'his, hers,' in the construction *ye-ʔad* 'his wife,' represents an unusual form of the third person possessive. The normal form of the third person possessive is *be-* 'his, hers.' The *ye-* form is used only when a possessor is not coreferential with the sentence subject. Such usages subordinate or "obviate" the discourse role of the possessor vis-à-vis the discourse role of the grammatical subject. In line 11 the storekeeper is referred to as a possessor. He is obviated with respect to the grammatical subject, Spencer. Moving down to line 14 we see this special possessive being used again, this time to "obviate" Spencer in a section in which the storekeeper is the primary focus. This special possessive, then, allows reference to be made to secondary actors in possessive constructions without undermining the organization of actor focus in that section of discourse.

A third element utilized to underscore continuity is direct discourse. Direct discourse is used to intensify the actor focus in segments II(ii), (iii), and (v). The passages quoted are not especially memorable or especially revealing. What seems to be critical is that the thoughts and words of the narrative actors be perceived as direct expressions. Narrative direct discourse is never used to shift focus; it is used to reinforce, or intensify, actor focus within narrative episodes.

A fourth element is evident in situations in which secondary actors act upon the primary actor. Linguists have come to expect unusual constructions in this situation (Silverstein 1976). In Algonquian, for example, the famous inverse construction appears in this situation. Recall that in Algonquian languages, secondary actors are indicated with what is called an obviative suffix. When the primary actor acts on a secondary actor, the verb is in its normal or direct form. When a secondary actor, marked as an obviative, acts on the primary actor, however, the verb is conjugated in the inverse (for details, see Dahlstrom 1992).

The construction that occurs under these same circumstances in Chilcotin, which for the moment I will call the obviating plural, shares some of the properties of Algonquian inverses. In normal third person–to–third person transitive constructions in Chilcotin, the subject is indicated with a ɸ- 'he, she' attached directly to the stem. The direct object is indicated with a *yi-* 'him, her,' which is attached to the left of aspect and mode prefixes and also to the left of the subject. In the obviating plural construction, the subject is indicated with the plural *ji-* 'they,' and the order in which the arguments is expressed is reversed: the plural subject pronoun appears to the left of the object *yi-* 'him, her.' Thus, this represents not merely the substitution of one (obviating) subject marker for another; this also represents a special type of inverse grammatical construction.

The construction is evident on line 28. Spencer is the primary actor throughout this section. In line 28, "The storekeeper, he had found out," the storekeeper is represented as the agent and the sentence subject. The use of the plural obviative construction, *jégughintan* 'he had found that out,' allows for the representation of a secondary actor as the subject without upsetting the organization of participant relations in the discourse. In this way it reinforces continuity of actor hierarchy in the discourse. Another example occurs in line 71, in a section in which Spencer is the primary actor. The construction appears when a secondary actor in the section plays the part of agent and sentence subject: "when he [Jerry] found him [Spencer]."

In line 81 Johnny initiates the account of the first cattle. This narrative is marked section III on the transcript. The first section begins by reestablishing the setting. These events occurred slightly earlier in time because the central figure *ʔeyen desaghint'i* 'must have been him,' that is, must have been Spencer, who was still alive then. And they occurred "around here." Given that there were not many animals in the valley at that time and the grass was tall, Spencer sensed an opportunity to exploit what he saw as free range: "He [Spencer] herded them [his cattle] to this area after the winter."

The perspective changes at this point to center on Sam Richard, famous early resident of Nemiah Valley and, as it happens, Johnny's father. Sam tries to warn Spencer off. However, he does not do so by claiming title to the land. Rather, he indicates that a local spirit, Tsil'os, a mountain that was once a man, will chase Spencer off: *ʔéyed Tsil'os, bígwení . . . bígweníjed hánt'áh* 'that [inanimate] *Tsil'os*, he'll frighten you . . . he'll frighten you for certain. . . !' As William Abraham told me in when I first arrived, Tsil'os is believed to use the weather to his own purposes. "Watch yourself!" Sam Richard continues. There is no indication of Spencer's reaction, and in this case, silence speaks volumes. We imagine Spencer continuing on and Sam Richard fatalistically standing by, and we are reminded of Melville Jacobs's characterization of the central preoccupation of historical narratives of the Pacific Northwest:

Indians . . . would not think of forcibly halting a person who had advanced in the direction of a denouement that was certain death. Such respect for other persons' choices, such conviction that they could not and would not listen to advice to be cautious, such fatalism from the point of view of Western ideology, are alien to most Euroamericans. Such policy expressed acceptance of a tragic destiny, in a frame of proper northwest states' Indian etiquette, values, and orientation about people's self-identities. They were unchangeably what they were. They did what they did. Their direction was unalterable. Nothing could change such people, such events, such reality. (1968:188–189)

A narratee experienced in the ways of historical narrative would expect, then, that Spencer was headed for trouble.

Before continuing, Johnny reaffirms that the man known as Sam Richard, who attempted to warn Spencer, was his late father. This section is parallel to section II(vi) of the first narrative, in which, after continued focus on the antics of non-Indians, the narrative line shifts to Jerry, the Anaham man who happened to live in the area the men entered. Here again the narrative line shifts to an Indian man who happens to live in the area that a non-Indian is entering. It is different in that this time the area featured in the narrative is the same one in which the account is being narrated and different in that the Indian man in question is not only named but also happens to be a close relative and the likely source of the entire account. In other words, Sam Richard represents what Wayne Booth calls a dramatized narrator, albeit a disguised one:

We should remind ourselves that many dramatized narrators are never explicitly labeled as narrators at all. In a sense, every speech, every gesture, narrates; most works contain disguised narrators who are used to tell the audience what it needs to know, while seeming merely to act out their roles.

Though disguised narrators of this kind are seldom labeled so explicitly as God in Job, they often speak with an authority as sure as God's. Messengers returning to tell what the oracle said, wives trying to convince their husbands that the business deal is unethical, old family retainers expostulating with wayward scions—these often have more effect on us than on their official auditors; the king goes ahead with his obstinate search, the husband carries out his deal, the hell-bound youth goes on toward hell as if nothing had been said, but we know what we know—and as surely as if the author himself or his official narrator had told us. (1996:148)

Dramatized narrators, in other words, represent the author's presence from the point of view of narrative action. Thus, they provide critical links between narrating events and narrated events.

Transliterating Booth's comments on written fiction so that they apply to oral narrative, one might say that in every narrative experience there is an implied dialogue among speech event narrator (Booth's *author*), narrated event narrator (Booth's *narrator*), actors (Booth's *characters*), and speech event narratee (Booth's *reader*). Booth observes: "Each of the four can range in relation to each of the others, from identification to complete opposition, on any axis of value, moral intellectual, aesthetic, and even physical" (1996:150). In this episode, the narrator identifies with the narrated event narrator, who is dramatized, of course, by an actor in the narrative. It remains for the narratees to resolve their own relation with each of the other elements, but the speech event narrator has managed relations between narrating and narrating events in such a way as to offer two possibilities:

Jerry : Sam Richard : Johnny Richard : : Spencer : non-Indians around there : narratee

or

Jerry : Sam Richard : Johnny Richard : narratee : : Spencer : non-Indians from around there.

Which is it going to be?

Developing a sense for the unfolding of the "reading" experience from the point of view of a hypothetical narratee requires that we consider the relations between the two narratives in more detail The first part of the first narrative alternates exclusively between two non-Chilcotin individuals, Spencer and the storekeeper. But in section II(vi) the Chilcotin people enter the picture, so to speak, to help locate a body that happened into their territory. Jerry finds it because of another morally loaded attribute of Spencer's, his practice of wearing a diamond ring. Johnny suggested to me several days after he presented this account that Jerry received a $200 reward for discovering the body. Thus, while the tension between the two historical frames—Indians around here and non-Indians around there—suggested at the outset of the narrative event is eclipsed by actions within the realm of non-Indians around there, the shift out of the blue to a focus on the Chilcotin man Jerry and the accumulated sense that all that resulted from Spencer's bizarre activities were his death and an incremental improvement (a $200 reward) in conditions for "the Indians around here" suggest that it is too soon to dismiss the Indians around here.

The organization of this narrative can be represented (where ~A means *not A*) to highlight the poetic-logical relations among subsections:

(i)   A

(ii)   B

(iii)   A

(iv)   B

(v)   A

(vi)   C

(vii)   A′

(viii)   ~A

Representing the organization of the second narrative in the same way highlights the dependence of the latter on the former:

(i)   A

(ii)   C′

(iii)   A′

(iv)   ~A

(v)   C″

If we disregard for the moment the very last section, we can see that the pattern of the second narrative recapitulates the pattern of the second half of the first narrative. Each moves from a focus on Spencer, to a focus on Indians from around here, to Spencer's possessions, to a section that presents the resolution as the resumption of a state of affairs in which Spencer plays no part.

The parallel between the structures of the two narratives is first brought into the narratee's field of view in section III(ii), which as we know, centers on Sam Richard warning Spencer. The sections that follow are critical for shaping the direction of association so that it runs from second narrative, to first narrative, to speech event. Section III(iii) describes the destruction of Spencer's cows in an avalanche, along the lines predicted by Bulyan. Section III(iv) emphasizes the extent to which these events resulted in Spencer becoming a nonentity "around here": "That is all he did, he did not return this way." At this point the parallels between the poetics of the two narratives are unmistakable.

In the final section Johnny counterposes a thought of a narrative actor, Spencer's "I'm going to land grab here," with what is apparently an observation of his own as speech event narrator, namely, that "he couldn't do that at all, much land . . . , Tsil'os spoiled it for him." However, insofar as the observation captures the perlocutionary (see Austin 1962) effect of Sam Richard's earlier speech act of warning, it represents the complete convergence of the speech event narrator and the dramatized narrator. This closure of distance between participants in the narrating and narrated events serves as the final model for the narratee to effect the same. The preferred association at this point is unmistakably

> Spencer : non-Indians from around there : : Jerry : Sam Richard
> : Johnny Richard : narratee.

Conclusion

The first variety of history I encountered at Nemiah Valley was historical narrative practice, and this was probably not incidental. It is a historical variety that seems to have filled the need to address those interventions between past and present introduced by such outsiders as Spencer. It is a variety with considerable utility in structuring a historical disjuncture of a certain sort, the one introduced by the arrival of entrepreneurs. This explains in part why Johnny Richard was less mortified by the self-serving way I elicited the narrative than I am when I think back on it. He expected me to act as the generic protagonists do, without a clear understanding for, or appreciation of, Chilcotin protocol. In a sense, the behavior I exhibited is exactly what these sorts of narratives are meant to address. The narrative fit the occasion, or rather, the occasion fit the narrative. And the occasion fit the narrative when William Abraham first presented it to Terry Glavin and me at his temporary camp. We had just entered the valley to work on our "projects." For our benefit and his, he put us into meaningful relations with some fellow "entrepreneurs" from the community's past.

In one sense these narratives represent specific incidents, and each incident seems to have its own significance. In another sense they might be taken as a whole to represent historical change in structural terms. When outsiders came to the valley they consciously or unconsciously brought new forms of economic and political organization. They effectively changed the social environment. These historical narratives exhibit Chilcotin cultural perspectives on how to go about addressing new situations, from the incursion of ranchers, to the ineptitudes of anthropologists, to the behavior of younger generations.

What had William intended by the account? It certainly confirmed the role Tsil'os plays in the area. It was a warning of sorts for Terry and me. It was also in a sense a warning for other anthropologists. But given the occasion and the characteristics of the genre as sketched out above, William was essentially addressing a set of historical circumstances that we happened into. He was exerting his influence over a historical conjuncture.

The most prevalent approaches to narrative text, structural analysis and ethnopoetics, however, are poorly suited to this material. They help considerably in identifying those aspects of narrative structure that transcend the moment, but they cannot help us see why people feel that these structures are especially relevant to one situation or another. The performance approach helps us understand the responsibilities and achievements of performers vis-à-vis audience members but fails to help us understand why relations between these parties are not addressed directly. The approach best suited to this material, then, is one that provides for an integrated overarching view of the process of narrative entextualization and contextualization (Bauman and Briggs 1990; Silverstein and Urban 1996). Historical scenarios are activated part by part. Each part emphasizes particular role relations. This sequence presents a course of identification that moves from the imaginary to the necessary, from the possible to the essential. The conjuncture is "structured" in the prosaics of narrative.

Postscript

In Keith Basso's examples of Western Apache historical tales (1996) actors are not named; nor is identity specified in any way other than "a man" or "a woman." No names are given, and no mention is made of how actors are related to the narrator. The central actors in Chilcotin historical tales, on the other hand, are almost always named. They are named, and they happen to be people that many of the elder generation actually knew.

Not only are central actors named in Chilcotin historical tales, but typically some account is made of how the narrator came to hear of the events in question. Typically, the events were witnessed in some fashion by a kin relative who related the account to the present narrator.

These stylistic differences are suggestive of significant differences in the nature of relations between narrated and narrating events in the two parallel renditions. In both their full and their abbreviated forms, Western Apache historical tales direct Apache individuals to, as Basso puts it,

> travel in your mind to a point from which to view the place whose name has just been spoken. Imagine standing there, as if in the tracks of your ancestors, and recall stories of events that occurred at that place long ago. Picture these events in your mind and appreciate, as if the ancestors were speaking to you directly, the knowledge the stories contain. Bring this knowledge to bear on your own disturbing situation. Allow the past to inform your understanding of the present. You will feel better if you do. (1996:91)

Those who respond accordingly and who successfully travel in their minds "to a point from which to view the place whose name has just been spoken" come to hear and, in a sense, come to inhabit what Basso calls *the eyewitness voice* (1996:13). Nancy Munn's comments on the temporal significance of Apache historical tales further clarify their function:

> *In Apache narrations (8), ancestral place names orient listeners' minds to "look 'forward' into space," thus positioning them to "look 'backward' into time." Names identify "viewing points" "in front of places; 'as persons imagine themselves standing in front of a named site, they may imagine [themselves] . . . standing in their ancestors tracks' " (8:112). By taking the ancestor's position, a viewer transforms an ancestral "there-then" (what was for the ancestor, of course, a "here-now" of travel) into his/her own "here-now." Incorporated into the latter-day viewer's biography, ancestral events then become a particular form of "lived history" in Halbwachs's (78:43) sense. Coordinately, "A [specific] past [becomes] charged with the time of the now" (13:261), which also implies that it is charged with the expectancies or "possible futures" entailed in the "now." The time of the viewer, and that of the relevant landscape spaces with their ancestral meaning, "are being [mutually] refashioned in this process." (1992:113)*

In Chilcotin historical tales, on the other hand, people are often on the spot, or near the spot, where the historical events occurred. In effect, they do not "travel" in geographical space; they travel in genealogical space from "social relationship present" to "social relationship past" and then back.

3. Contemporary Myth

The tendency to assimilate others' discourse takes on an even deeper and more basic significance in an individual's ideological becoming, in the most fundamental sense. Another's discourse performs here no longer as information, directions, rules, models and so forth—but strives rather to determine the very bases of our ideological interrelations with the world.

M. M. Bakhtin (1981)

William Abraham was on the move again. He had flown to Vancouver for a cataract operation. Due to the wonders of Canadian national health care, the government had paid for his round-trip airfare from Williams Lake. When he had returned to Williams Lake, he had apparently taken the opportunity to visit friends and relatives in the area. At a certain point news reached Nemiah Valley that he had been seen in Williams Lake. But several more days passed, and he failed to come home as expected. His family was quietly concerned. Though it was not unusual for William to dally with friends and relatives on trips to town, the surgery was his first. He was getting older. This trip seemed different. More time passed, and people began to wonder whether he was coming back at all.

Terry Glavin had left the valley in late November. In December I had left the valley myself to spend Christmas with my parents in Montana. I returned to the valley in early January, wondering whether I would be remembered. I learned that I had bounced checks to the band and the local store. I was not only remembered, people were actively tracking me down. To my surprise the bounced checks led not to resentment but to no more than a little teasing. As one person explained to me, that happens to everybody.

Daniel had assumed temporary proprietorship of the house that Terry Glavin and I had originally been housed in. The man who actually owned it had left the reserve years before, and it was the only house on the reserve not in use. With the end of his employment on the book project Daniel was looking for a way to support himself. Having taught it in school, he was recognized as a specialist in the language. He was also a gifted musician and composed songs in his native language. He was, in short, a sort of philosopher-poet. Given his obvious talents and inclinations, I offered to pay a wage for linguistic consultation. Given my limited resources, the wage was modest ($10/hour). Nevertheless, he accepted. It would help pay the bills. And as long as I helped with groceries, propane, and firewood, he would let me stay in the house as well.

The house was located at a small settlement along the main road near the center of the valley in an area known as *tl'ebayi* 'level field.' Because most of the houses in the valley were further west, many people drove by our house on the way in or out of town. Daniel was gregarious, and people—Daniel's relatives, local children, and elders, sometimes looking for a conversation, oftentimes looking for a taxi ride—were constantly stopping to visit. People would often appear around noon for lunch and coffee. Nights, however, were generally quiet.

On the night of 20 January 1991, several weeks after he had been expected, William appeared out of the dark. I had been away that afternoon, helping a man drag a dead moose out of the woods. When I returned I found Daniel cooking Ramen noodles for William. One look and my worries about William's health were dispelled. His bright eyes radiated the restless energy of the road. As he slurped down the noodles, he indicated to me that he would appreciate a ride to his home at the west end of the valley. But first he wanted to talk to our neighbor, his brother-in-law and fellow elder, Erving. He quickly finished his noodles and disappeared into the night. Daniel soon followed. I ate quickly and followed as well. My impressions upon arrival at Erving's house are preserved in my notes:

> *I drove over when I finished. . . . When I arrived Erving and William sat on the couch together. Daniel sat next to a window, facing north, facing the stove. William sat next to Erving on the couch, almost as though he were leaning on Erving's huge shoulder.*
>
> *Erving is very large, nearly a foot and a half taller than William, who he calls, "Abraham." Erving leaned back, as he typically does, on the southern end of his couch. [This was the privileged seat in the house. I had sat there next to Erving on other occasions, one time in particular when we two and Erving's son Conrad were watching* WWF *wrestling through the electric snow of a small (four-inch screen) battery-powered television set.]*
>
> *When I first arrived they interpreted some of what they were saying to me in English. After a bit though they seemed to assume I would understand. I could at least make out the topic. They were trading stories about ghosts and about Lejab 'the Devil.' These seem to be favorite topics. Erving referred to William as "oldtimer" for me, as if to explain his interest in William's talk. And Erving, though he told some stories, listened for the most part.*

At a certain point William and Erving became more serious. William launched into an extended narrative about a man's journey to and from the land of the dead. I could follow well enough to know that the account was unusual. I had not heard it or anything quite like it to this point in my stay. Animated discussion followed. Eventually, they returned to less involved subjects:

> *I could hear a few places and names.* Labusten *came up. Erving talked about the graveyard near his house and one at Stoney reserve. The topic changed then to Erving's brother's pickup which was being repaired at Alexis Creek. The whereabouts of his brother and who had driven him where during his journey were thoroughly discussed. The topic changed to the price of hay and the fact that William had just bought 300 bales at two dollars a bale from George Smith (a non-Indian rancher in the valley). Finally after several cigarettes and cups of* ledi *'tea' William was ready to go. In Chilcotin Erving told us we might meet a tall man (on our journey through the dark), referring again to Lejab.*

Afterward Daniel and I drove roughly eight miles to William's house at the west end of the valley and left him at the door. We returned home and turned in for the evening, each of us in our way still wondering about William's account. Daniel was wondering about deeper meanings. I was wishing that I was better versed in the Chilcotin language.

Myth Analysis: State of the Art

It might seem plausible to suggest, given what we have seen to this point, that interpreting myths might require less reference to context than analyzing historical narratives. Certainly this idea is present in the ethnopoetics literature. Whether we accept Jarold Ramsey's statement that Dell Hymes's ethnopoetic analysis of myth and tale recitation in the Pacific Northwest as represented in *"In Vain I Tried to Tell You"* (1981) is "the single most penetrating analysis of a body of text materials in the Native American Literature" (from the book jacket) or not, there is no question that ethnopoetics sets the standard for the analysis of myth narrative, especially in the Pacific Northwest. According to Hymes, myths are delivered in a more formal style than tales. In other words, they exhibit the poetic properties of the tradition to the highest degree (Hymes 1981:171). Thus myth texts are identifiable, in the absence of other indications, on the basis of the presence of a high degree of formal regularity of text.

Working essentially with ethnographic and linguistic records of the traditional past, Hymes's analysis was guided by two interdependent principles: "that there is a consistent structure, and that it is to be found in terms of form-meaning covariation" (1981:151). In the Chinookan narrative tradition

Hymes has identified five levels of textual organization—act, scene, stanza, verse, and line:

All levels of organization of the text (line, verse, stanza, scene, act) show relations between content and linguistic form, but the relations vary in directness and consistency. It is the verse that is directly and consistently marked by a single, definable set of linguistic features, namely, sentence-initial particles. Verses in turn provide the frame within which lines are identifiable, and the element whose groupings provide for stanzas, and through stanzas, scenes. In the latter cases there is some direct marking by (or correlation with) linguistic features, but most of the relation to linguistic features derived from, and depends on, the patterning of lower level units, ultimately verses. (1981:151)

As he observes, the patterning of verses provides the basis for identifying all other levels of patterning.

Robert Moore has recently argued that mythological practice is not now, and perhaps never was, as oriented to the fashioning of text, poetic or otherwise, as ethnopoetics presumes. He argues that mythological practice is in fact geared to articulating relations between text and context. Drawing on the work of David French, Moore argues that "myth-telling" traditionally assumed two forms among the Wascos and Wishrams, "the FORMAL presentation of a mythical story or a cycle of myths," on the one hand, and "the casual use of myth materials at a time when the speaker is principally engaged in discussing something else" (French 1958:259–260, quoted in Moore in press:17), on the other. According to French, the formal presentation of mythical stories had disappeared already in the 1950s.

Moore argues that the practices of narrators with whom he himself worked, including Lucinda Smith, and those of many other narrators recorded by anthropologists represent the refinement of the tradition of informal, situationally intricate "sampling" of myth materials. He argues moreover that even in "their earlier modality as ritual narrations that literally moved the community of tellers and listeners toward springtime . . . recitals still depended for their efficacy on the very principles of contextualization" utilized in the extemporaneous informal practices (2000:19). Myth recitation today is distinguished by narrators acting on their own initiative outside of the context of formal ritual to contextualize everyday events by setting them into meaningful relation with mythical scenarios, through suggestion, commentary, narrative, and spontaneous theater, in short, through a creative, multimodal art of performance "often elicited by the activities of anthropologists as well as by casual conversation among Indians" (French 1958:260, quoted in Moore in press:17).

Evidence from Nemiah Valley, where myths are rarely presented as such but are introduced indirectly, sometimes surreptitiously, into daily life to accentuate certain moments, confirms Moore's intuitions regarding the orientation of myth-telling to context rather than text per se. And yet as stated his suggested revisions in ethnopoetics fail to account for two dimensions of the Chilcotin practices. First, even in extemporaneous indirect form, myth-like narrations exhibit to a remarkable degree the formal intricacies of central interest to ethnopoetics. This might be accounted for by suggesting that these properties are emphasized to ritualize situations of daily life. Second, again, even in extemporaneous indirect form, myth narratives bring to the situations in which they are narrated a gravity bordering on the sacred. These factors do not invalidate Moore's insights into the context dependency of myth narration in any way, but they suggest that while both are context dependent, historical narratives and mythical narratives seem to diverge in terms of formal patterning and in terms of the felt gravity of the situations in which they are presented.

Recording the Narrative

I made no recording of William's narrative when he first told it. I had no tape recorder at the time, and if I had, I would like to think that I would not have risked interrupting the narrative by attempting to record it. I simply tried to understand what I could. As it happened I was able to record a version of the account some time later. It is perhaps worth dwelling briefly on how that came to pass. On 4 February 1991, two weeks after Daniel and I had witnessed William presenting his account to Erving, I observed the following in my field notes:

> Several days after I returned from Montana, Daniel, one morning, began to marvel at a dream his father, William, had recounted to him while I was away. In the dream William gets lost in the woods and finally wanders into a small open area in a very brushy place. Daniel told me the name of the place, though I do not remember it ("brushy place" was a direct translation I believe).
>
> A number of people sat in the open area. I think Daniel said William recognized several old-timers. At least one woman was present, maybe William's grandmother. As William interpreted it, these people were dead and "serving time" in a sort of purgatory before moving on to heaven. When they saw him they asked what he was doing there. "Your time has not come, what are you doing here, you are not supposed to be here," they said.

*After relating his father's dream Daniel told me that a man
once entered a cave up near Bull Canyon. He told me a version of
the account.*

Now I cannot be sure as to when Daniel related his father's dream to me. Was
it before the night of his return or after? I obviously recorded this after, but I
indicate that I was remembering something that had happened not the day
before but a few days after I had returned from Montana. In any case, talk of
perilous journeys and visits to the land of the dead were in the air from the
time I returned. My notes indicate that even I was dimly aware of this.

At about 10:30 A.M., 14 February 1991, Daniel and I drove to William's
house with the express purpose of recording a narrative in the Chilcotin language to use for data for linguistic analysis. After I asked him about other
matters, William's earlier account of the man's journey to the land of the
dead came to mind, and I asked William whether he would mind recording
the account. Here I quote from my field notes of the occasion, written the
following day:

> *Yesterday, Daniel and I drove up to his parents' house at* lhizbay
> *(name for an area at the west end of Nemiah Valley) hoping to
> talk with his father about old times.*
>
> *We found William home with his wife Mary, his sons Billy and
> Jerold. We had encountered Denny (another son) and his wife
> Nancy and their family on the road. They had just lost their
> exhaust pipe. We laid the long exhaust pipe in my open trunk and
> took it to William's.*
>
> *Mary's son Harold (to another man) was just leaving as we
> arrived. His wife Molly had just cleaned William and Mary's
> house. When we entered Billy was working at the kitchen table
> trying to fix a cracked battery with Crazy Glue. William was also
> sitting at the table. I did my best to help.*
>
> *When we finished I set up my tape recorder in front of William.
> William was thinking about the upcoming funeral. Everyone was
> apparently passing the time hoping for news about the proceed-
> ings. William was especially interested in whether people would be
> gambling that evening at the dance hall.*
>
> *As I began to talk to William, Billy came over and we chatted
> about the tape recorder. Then I asked William about pit houses,
> something Daniel and I had been wondering about. He said he
> had never actually seen an authentic one, only one built by
> a trapper. When I asked whether his grandmother stayed in*

*one, he began talking about her moving out of them during the
smallpox.*

*Daniel had left the room as had the others and I was alone with
William for some time. He spoke in English. When he finished
I told him Daniel and I were trying to record some stories in
Chilcotin. I asked about a story he had told one night at Erving
Richard's house, an account of a man exploring a cave near Bull
Canyon.*

William began talking and soon Daniel returned to the room.

The tape shows that once I introduced my interest in the account, I prompted
the account with a somewhat enthusiastic burst of questions:

David: *Remember over at Erving's, you were talking about—
uhm—a guy over there by Bull Canyon, I think, that went in
and found a cave, he went in there. I wonder if you could tell
that one* nenqayni cheh?

William: *Uh huh. You batteries gonna be alright?*

[I check to see whether the recorder is working.]

D: *There was some guy? Do you know who that guy was—that
went in the cave?*

W: *No, but ah, like ah, I don't know the name but . . . but she
went . . . he was hunting . . . like a long time ago used to be just
black bear, that's all they eat. You want to go by* nenqayni?

D: *Yes.*

William began his narration in English, only checking to see which language
I preferred after he had finished laying out the premise. In retrospect I
wonder whether his question regarding which language I preferred was an
attempt to clarify my motivations. He knew I had been present when he had
given Erving the account in Chilcotin. If I had not understood the account
in Chilcotin, then why would I want it in Chilcotin now? Conversely, if I had
understood it then, why was I asking to hear it again? What was I interested
in, exactly? At the time, I was only interested in a narrative and was not
sensitive to the distinctions he seems to have been wondering about. What
the circumstances suggest is that William was aware of the possibility that I
was not interested in the account for my own sake alone.

The presence of his son Daniel at both events was a factor as well. From
the point at which he clarified which language I preferred, William seems to
have presented the account as though we were interested in what he had
presented at Erving's house.

David French observes that the "less formal use of myth materials continues today, and is often elicited by the activities of anthropologists as well as by casual conversation among Indians" (1958:260, quoted in Moore in press:17). The occasion for the "original" presentation of this narrative was a casual conversation among Indians; the occasion for its recording, the activities of an anthropologist. It is perhaps worth emphasizing, then, that the circumstances, and William's behaviors, underscore Moore's concern with the significance of context in the performance of myth narratives.

The Transcript

The transcript of the body of the narration has been arranged to highlight the difference between interpretive commentary oriented to participants in the immediate speech event (left column), the narrative line (indented once), and dialogue and commentary set within the narrated events (indented twice). The text has been organized into four sections, a prelude and three major units, to be discussed further below:

Prelude

Yedanx ʔegúh, sedanx,
'Long ago, before my time'
ses dza dzíyan nenduwh nench'ed . . . han,
'they ate only bear in this area,'
guyen ses qayítísdzáh
'they hunted for bear'
lhin nánqí bélh xélhʔés, sántih.
'with two dogs going along, must have been.'

5   *Ses tenayug gwéqa ʔeguh nayelhdilh.*
'They brought them for chasing the bears.'

Gu Gwetsilh gwech'anlgáy,
'He departed afoot [walked away] from Gwetsilh,'
ʔegun lha deni ghenénádál.
'the man did not return [walk back].'
Ch'íz lha ʔagúséd ghili,
'Not a little later,'
ʔán beqa ts'ezʔíz ʔan.
'they searched for him.'

10   *Lha . . . lha nentsin gughinyeh cheguyeh.*
'Did not . . . they did not realize where [he had gone].'

I

ʔegun ʔech'an guxéljid ʔeguh,
'Then when he first crawled inside,'

lha ʔagúnséd hénljíd.
'he crawled not a little distance.'
ʔegun guyi dzax gánt'í daghínk'en,
'Then where that sort of burnt pitch,'
ʔeyi diláx yénágháljíd,
'when he crawled to where that lay,'
15   naxaghílhjíd.
'he crawled back.'
Guyí belin,
'His dogs,'
        "ʔéyí batintaxaghúnálh xagaghezlawz,"
       ' "they might wander off," '
[yenizen].
[he thought].
Ses gha lhin yít'ín,
'He had those dogs for (hunting) bears,'
20   *ʔí(yen).*
'that man.'
        Shúnchúh shúnchúh ʔegun belin jidáxíztl'un nah.
'Again, again, then he tied his dogs up.'
Yedanx lhá tl'ulh ts'est'in,
'Long ago they did not have rope,'
gán guyi ts'ax gánt'í tl'ulh ts'it'in.
'but they had that sinew kind of rope.'
Nulhts'ez ts'ílhchúg ʔegúh sés táh.
'From animals it was taken, bear and others.'
25   *ʔeyi gant'i chu bid jidayaghéztl'ún.*
'With that very kind he tied them up.'
II(a)
        Shúnchúh ch'ah gúnághaljid.
'And again he crawled back.'
ʔank'án ʔílhés yánáh talgwelh ʔájá
'But very far he would crawl'
        "ʔegun, gun ses hets'élish,"
       ' "where they bring bears out," '
gunízlíd dáh.
'he thought.'
30   *ʔaghúlhts'én hátin ʔana (santih).*
'It must have been spring.'
        ʔégun hínk'an ʔiyed dzáx daghínk'án
'And then at the burned pitch'

gúʾén ghelgwelh gát'in.
'he crawled further.'
Chilhʾanz hínk'an duwh gagunt'íh
'Later, at a place like this'
gan yeqox nílín,
'but where there was a river,'

35   tsi yeqox,
'a rocky river,'
ʾegun haghéljíd.
'he crawled out.'
ʾeyí nen yax gunán tsi ch'ed
'On that land on the other side on a rock'
nájádílhʾin.
'he spotted them.'
Guts'én yánish hink'an
'As he (was crawling) out'

40   lha jíd jíyéduts'án gulah,
'they could not hear him at all,'
lha chadesnax.
'he was not dead yet.'

(b)

ʾegúh ʾilhanx yádish gwénen,
'Then a person far up there on the side,'
belhadínlh ts'á,
'when he [the man] yawned,'
ʾegun ʾelhch'enast'iz,
'opened his eyes,'

45   yádish gwenen ʾegun,
'way up there then,'
ts'éⁱzdax deniʲ hinlhtsan.
'the manʲ spotted someoneⁱ [the man] sitting.'
ʾegúh hínk'an jiyets'en xenínan.
'At that moment they went toward him.'
     "ʾank'an, lha ch'adézínax ʾeguh,
     ' "So now, since you have not died yet,'
     "lha jíd nénján nághúyá gúláh,"
     ' "you cannot walk around here at all," '

50   jiyelhnah."
'they told him.'

One dáy dza ʔagháťín yenizen, fíve yéars hághínli.
'He thought only one day had passed, but it was five years.'
Chuh lhá guyenizil,
'Still he did not realize,'
guyen deni. Heh heh.
'that man. Heh heh.'

(c)

ʔegúh hínk'an,
'Pretty soon then,'

55 "ch'áh,"
' "[you must go] back," '
jighénánezíltan.
'they explained to him.'
"ʔegúh ch'adínjágh
' "When you die'
"nenján tághendalh,"
' "you will live here," '
jiyelhni han.
'they told him.'

60 "Lha ch'adazínax,
' "You have not died yet,'
"lha jid ghundá gúláh.
' "so you cannot live here at all.'
"Gan ch'ah,"
' "But [you must go] back," '
jighanánézaíltan.
'they explained.'
"Yax ch'áh
' "To get back,'

65 "gwexénághíljid."
' "you crawl out there." '
ʔegúh, ʔegúh gwexenághíljid,
'When, when he crawled out,'
guyí belin qanáťís,
'he searched for his dogs,'
ʔegwed gásh dza ʔeguh dizdzi.
'[there were] only bleached bones piled together.'

III

ʔegúh hink'an,
'Then,'

70   yax Gwetsilh natilhgay,
       'he walked to Gwetsilh,'
       ʔí(yen),
       'that one.'
ʔank'an guyen ch'adejagh ts'iyenizen
'But they thought that one had died.'
deni ghenanághálgay ʔeskulá xi haghinlí.
'When he returned (walking) to the people it had been five years.'
Beʔad ʔiyén sunk'ah ʔiyed sedax.
'She who was his wife was still living there.'
75 *ʔandza lhuwí ninlagh ʔeguh gwexánáljid.*
'He crawled out of there just when the fish were plentiful.'
    lhuwi ʔanádzálí ʔegúh ʔiyed ghananaghálgay.
    'They were harvesting fish when he arrived there.'
    Lha nents'ez xanághájeh chuh guts'iyénizen,
    'They did not even know where he came from,'
    gan gats'in jiyehughízdíl
    'but they all gathered round him'
    jíyúdelhqed:
    'and questioned him:'
80   "ʔegúh nen gágúnt'éh
      ' "It was a land like this'
      "ʔégúh xaghesjid,
      ' "that I crawled out of,'
      "ʔilhed dziny dza xaghat'in yenesen,
      ' "I thought it was one day,'
      "guchuh five years haghinli,
      ' "still it was five years,'
      "lha guyenesinl,"
      ' "I never realized," '
85   *ni.*
      'he said.'
  Heh heh, yeah.

"Walking" through the Text

William begins with the formulaic phrase, "Long ago, before my time." He then fills in background information regarding the nature of those times, perhaps for the benefit of the incompletely socialized anthropologist: "they ate only bear in this area, they hunted for bear with two dogs. . . . They brought them for chasing the bears."

He initiates the narrative per se in line 6, focusing on the actions of "the man": "He departed afoot [walked away] from Gwetsilh." In line 7 he shifts to the perspective of the villagers: "The man did not return [walk back]. Not a little later, they searched for him." William then explains, "Did not . . . they did not realize where [he had gone]." By indicating that the man "did not return" without indicating where he had gone, and by adding that "they did not realize where he had gone," William foreshadows the unusual character of the man's journey.

At this point (line 11) William dispenses with the complexities of preliminary framing and enters the mainstream of the third person perfect narrative: "Then when he first crawled inside, he crawled a little distance. Then where that sort of burnt pitch, when he crawled to where that lay, he crawled back." As part of the narrative action, he introduces the first segment of direct discourse: "His dogs, 'They might wander off,' [he thought]."

He then steps away from the narrative line to remind his narratees again why the man had the dogs: "He had those dogs for [hunting] bears, that man." William reenters the narrative and completes the scene ("Again, again, then he tied his dogs up"), then steps away again to explain how the man could have tied the dogs up without rope: "Long ago they did not have rope, but they had that sinew kind of rope. From animals it was taken, bear and others. With that very kind he tied them up."

William initiates the second part of the narrative by describing the man reentering the cave, this time to go as far as possible, " 'where they bring bears out,' he thought." William again steps out of the narrative to observe that the season must have been spring. He does this perhaps to remind us that bears were hunted while they were hibernating.

In line 31 he reenters the main stream of the narrative again: "And then at the burned pitch he crawled further. Later, at a place like this but where there was a river, a rocky river, he crawled out. On that land on the other side on a rock he spotted them." He spotted whom? we wonder. As the man approaches what seems to be a important group of people, William chooses to explain the situation only indirectly: "As he [was crawling] out they could not hear him at all." Why could they not hear him? They "could not hear him at all," William explains, "*he was not dead yet.*" As he suggests indirectly that the man is encountering distinctly unusual people, William brings the first section of the second part of his narrative to a close.

He initiates a second section with a narrative account of the encounter: "Then a person far up there on the side, when he [the man] yawned, opened his eyes, way up there then, the man[j] spotted someone[i] [the man] sitting. At that moment they went toward him." Here, then, is the encounter itself: " 'So now, since you have not died yet, you cannot walk around here at all,' they told him." William reinforces his indirect suggestions as to the strangeness of the encounter by stepping out of the narrative frame and observing to his narratees that, while the man thought he had been in the cave only one day, in fact he had been in there for five years: "Still, he did not realize."

He initiates the third section of the second part by bringing the narrative up to the crucial moment of the encounter. It would no doubt be unusual for anyone to leave the land of the dead. Would they make him stay? "Pretty soon then, '[you must go] back,' they explained to him. 'When you die you will live here,' they told him. 'You have not died yet, so you cannot live here at all. But [you must go] back,' they explained. 'To get back, you crawl out there.'" The man crawls out to find bleached bones where he expected living dogs. How long was he in the cave? we wonder.

William's account of the journey home from the cave makes up the third part of the narrative. It is initiated with a brief swatch of narrative discourse: "Then, he walked to Gwetsilh, that one." William then steps away from the narrative for a lengthy stretch of commentary, the longest, in fact, other than the prelude: "But they thought that one had died. When he returned [walking] to the people it had been five years. She who was his wife was still living there. He crawled out of there just when the fish were plentiful." If the man's encounter with the dead required little explanation, his encounter with his fellow villagers after his strange journey required much more.

William reenters the narrative: "They were harvesting fish when he arrived there. They did not even know where he came from, but they all gathered round him and questioned him: 'It was a land like this that I crawled out of, I thought it was one day, still it was five years, I never realized,' he said." Then, admiring the account, William responds as if he were a member of his own audience and laughs, "Heh heh, yeah."

Poetics of the Text

Verses are not so easily identified in this Chilcotin narrative as Hymes's work with Chinookan narratives suggests they might be. Verses cannot be identified on the basis of particle use alone. Consequently, I have begun by identifying lines on the basis of clauses or, in some cases, other grammatical constituents. Segmenting lines in this way, several patterns of line-end verb parallelism become apparent. One important parallel framework, for example, surrounds the verb "to walk."

The first usage of "to walk"—*Gu Gwetsilh gwech'anlgáy* 'He departed afoot [walked away] from Gwetsilh'—literally marks the opening of the narrative. The second usage, "the man did not return [walk back]," suggests that the narrative plot turns on whether the man *ever* returns. Consider the remaining narrative uses of the verb in sequence. As noted, the man *Gwetsilh gwech'anlgáy* 'departed afoot [walked away] from Gwetsilh' (line 6). The people he meets inside a cave tell him: *lha jíd nénján nághúyá gúláh* 'you cannot walk around here at all' (line 49). Reemerging from the cave, he *Gwetsilh natilhgay* 'walked to Gwetsilh' (line 70).

Viewed as a whole, the poetic distribution of the verb "to walk" provides the narrative account with an indexical envelope, demarcating the movement from here to there (*gwe*-ch'anlgáy 'walked away') and the movement from there to here (*na*-tilhgay 'walked back'). The distribution is presented here with indentation to highlight parallels, as the poetic structure a, b, c, a':

I	(a)	*Gu Gwetsilh gwech'anlgáy* 'He departed afoot [walked away] from Gwetsilh'
	(b)	*ʔegun lha deni ghenénádál* 'The man did not return [walk back]'
II	(c)	*"lha jíd nénján nághúyá gúláh," jiyelhnah* ' "You cannot walk around here at all," they told him'
III	(a')	*yax Gwetsilh natilhgay* 'he walked to Gwetsilh'

Recall that after walking to the cave, the man crawls inside. This act initiates a series of episodes of crawling back and forth through the cave. When he finally crawls out for the last time, he resumes walking for the duration of the account. Consequently, we can see that a poetics of "crawling" is embedded within the poetics of "walking":

I	1	*ʔegun ʔech'an guxéljid ʔeguh* 'when he first crawled inside'
	2	*lha ʔagúnséd hénljíd* 'he crawled not a little distance'
	3	*ʔegun . . . ʔeyi diláx yénágháljíd* 'when he crawled to where that lay'
	4	*naxaghílhjíd* 'he crawled back'
II(a)	5	*shúnchúh ch'ah gúnághaljid* 'and again he crawled back'

6 ˀank'án ˀílhés yánáh talgwelh ˀájá
  'but very far he would crawl'

7 gúˀén ghelgwelh gát'in
  'he crawled further'

8 tsi yeqox, ˀegun haghéljíd
  '[at] a rocky river, he crawled out'

II(b) 9 "Yax ch'áh gwexénághíljid"
   ' "To get back, you crawl out there" '

II(c) 10 ˀegúh gwexenághíljid
   'when he crawled out'

III 11 "ˀegúh nen gágúnt'éeh ˀégúh xaghesjid"
   ' "It was a land like this that I crawled out of" '

Initiated by the use of the phrase "crawled inside" and completed with the phrase "crawled out of," the poetics of "crawling" is set in parallel to the poetics of "walking," redoubling the recurrent poetic sound-meaning texture.

At the other extreme (act versus line) the narrative can be divided into four parts: a prelude, in which the narrative setting is introduced and the narrative action is previewed, and three segments, each of the latter being built around the dramatistic portrayal of an action or interaction. Borrowing Hymes's terminology, I will designate these dramatic segments *acts*. Acts can be further subdivided into scenes. Act II, the pivotal one, is divided into three scenes.

The most fundamental units in this Chilcotin narrative seem to be the acts. The focus of each act is the portrayal of a speech event. In Act I the man crawls into the cave. When he is well inside he thinks to himself that if he does not tie up his dogs, they will wander off. At this point this speech act, or "thought act," seems merely prudent.

The focus of each scene is a speech event as well. In Act II(a) the man crawls into the cave again and then reminds himself—in a speech act—that he will go farther this time: " 'where they bring bears out,' he thought." In Act II(b) the dead discover the man's presence and address him: " 'So now, since you have not died yet, you cannot walk around here at all,' they told him." In Act II(c) the dead explain the situation to the man, and they explain to him how to return to his own land: " '[You must go] back,' they explained to him. 'When you die, you will live here, they told him. 'You have not died yet, so you cannot live here at all, but [you must go] back,' they explained.

'To get back, you crawl out there.' " In Act III the villagers question the man (*jíyúdelhqed*), and he explains: "It was a land like this that I crawled out of, I thought it was one day, still it was five years, I never realized,' he said." Each act is thus built around the dramatization of a speech event, with one act being divided into three scenes, each of which is built around a speech event.

To summarize, although verses per se have proven to be more elusive than line-end parallelism and the differentiation of acts around dramatized speech events (see Moore 1993; Silverstein 1985; Urban 1984), this narrative nevertheless exhibits a high degree of aesthetic patterning, especially when contrasted with the historical narratives examined in chapter 2. The text is rich enough in recurrent poetic texture that whether it reaches the formal symmetry that ethnopoetics predicts or expects of myth, this is an aspect of its structure that cannot be discounted out of hand.

Poetics of Context

Notwithstanding his explicit claim that the man existed "before my time," William uses several techniques to indirectly reestablish an affinity between himself and the main actor in his narrative. One set of techniques is based in the representation of dialogue; that is, the portions of the narrative indented two steps to the right in the transcript. For example, in the final episode William recounts how upon his return the man's fellow villagers questioned him. He responded with an account of a journey to the land of the dead: "It was a land like this that I crawled out of. . . ." William thereby indirectly proffers an analogy between the circumstances surrounding the two narrative speech events:

the man's fellow villagers : the man as traveler-narrator : : William's fellow villagers : William as narrator.

A second technique based on the representation of dialogue is the way William portrays the main actor's thoughts and words. He portrays the man's thoughts and his verbal exchanges without any qualification, as though he has direct access to them (" 'They might wander off,' he thought"; " 'Where they bring bears out,' he thought"; " 'So now, since you have not died yet, you cannot walk around here at all"). It would not be out of the ordinary when quoting another's thoughts or verbal exchanges to indicate the source of this information; but William rather pointedly provides no such sources. This forces the narratee to wonder whether William knows the man's thoughts from personal experience.

A third technique bearing on the presentation of dramatic dialogue is the timing of the narrative performance. By performing his narrative (at Erving's house) upon his return from a perilous journey, just as the main character in the narrative had, William further underscores the analogy between the verbal activity in the narrated and the narrating scenarios:

the man's fellow villagers : traveler-narrator : : William's fellow villagers : traveler-narrator William.

A second set of techniques for managing relations between narrated and narrating scenarios, and thus another set of techniques for developing the poetics of context, is based in the commentary set in the immediate speech event (as represented in the transcript by the italicized speech at the left). The commentary is particularly useful for identifying the frames the narrator had in mind as the text is formulated. Commentary forms the bulk of the prelude. In it William specifies time and place and sketches out enough cultural background ("they ate only bear in this area, they hunted for bear with two dogs going along, must have been") that the narratee can follow the narrative. William also foreshadows the supernatural character of the events to follow.

Commentary in the first act centers on the dogs: why the man had them and what kind of rope he used to tie them up. Again, this might be viewed as cultural background. Commentary in the second act emphasizes the discontinuity between what was happening in fact and what was apparent to the man's senses at the time. For example, once the man is deep in the cave, William notes, "It must have been spring," presumably because people hunt for bears in caves in spring. The effect of his comment, however, is to call out attention to the limits of the man's perception. When the people he sees fail to sense his presence when he expects they should, William comments, "he was not dead yet." This confirms the narratee's impression that the man's senses are not tuned in to his actual surroundings. When the people inform the man that he should not be with them because he has not died yet, William comments that the man remains unaware of the nature of his predicament: "He thought only one day had passed, but it was five years." When he laughs at this discrepancy, William has assumed the role of audience, modeling the appropriate perlocutionary effect of the state of affairs in the narrative.

Commentary in the third act first reminds us of the discontinuity between the experience of the man and that of his fellow villagers. In the prelude William comments, "Did not . . . they did not realize where [he had gone]." In the final act, as the man returns to his village, William comments: "But they thought that one had died. When he returned [walking] to the people it had been five years." Then William emphasizes the fact that the two realms of sensory experience come back together: "She who was his wife was still living there. He crawled out of there just when the fish were plentiful." The man is there with her, and the fish are apparent to both. As a final bit of commentary, William laughs when the man indicates that he never realized what was going on. Again, William puts himself in the part of an audience member when he laughs, as though to direct our attention to what he thinks is remarkable about the account.

In sum, the commentary consists of three types: (1) noting discrepancies between the ontic realm assumed to be in play and the one actually in play, (2) adding necessary cultural background, and (3) laughing. Each is indicative of the frame William is applying to the narrating event. In the first type William assumes the role of an omniscient narrator, someone who can move back and forth between the then-and-there and the here-and-now in order to clarify the relations between the two. This sort of role presupposes the presence of a novice to the narrative tradition, one who is unable to see for oneself the implications of the narrative. In the second type William assumes the role of benevolent host. This role presupposes the presence of a novice to the cultural tradition, someone who is not aware of such basic facts about traditional culture as what people ate and what they used for rope. The third type, laughing, as noted above, indicates that William is assuming the role of narratee. This presupposes the presence of novices to the particular narrative in question, that is, people who are not sure what they are supposed to make of it.

As expected for an occasion of informal myth-telling, the commentary is substantial. It provides some evidence that when William recorded this account he was attentive to the necessity of assisting his audience. On the other hand, it is surprising how little of the commentary clearly presupposes the nearly completely naive audience present on the occasion the narrative was recorded. Of the three types of commentary, only the second, filling in cultural background, would necessarily indicate that William assumed he was narrating to a complete novice. And much of that type of commentary seems to be involved in literary techniques of narrative foreshadowing and highlighting. For example, the bulk of commentary that seems to be devoted to cultural background concerns the dogs, their presence, their number, and what was used to tie them up. This abundant commentary also serves the literary purpose of increasing our expectations regarding the role of the dogs in the plot, so that we are quite stunned when the man crawls out of the cave to find not dogs but only bleached bones.

This type of myth narration represents the informal application of a mythical scenario to the circumstances of daily life, though it exhibits some properties associated with full formal ritual narration. The content of the narrative informs us that the full ritual setting for this type of account is the occasion of reincorporation into the group following a perilous and supernaturally significant journey. Those circumstances were met remarkably closely when William presented his account to Erving. By performing the narrative upon his own return to the valley, William apparently ritualized what might otherwise have been seen as no more than "a casual conversation between Indians." Although the performance did not presuppose a ritual frame, in a real sense, it entailed one. Key to this entailment were the recurrent forms of poetic texture William imparted to his delivery. Thus, at one level this first narrative represents a conversation between friends one night on the reserve. At another it represents a formalization or ritualization of an otherwise mundane role, enabling "an individual's ideological becoming, in the most fundamental sense." Through the narration and the transformations it effected, the discourse "str[o]ve to determine the very bases of our ideological interrelations with the world" (Bakhtin 1981:342).

Conclusion

I encountered the variety of historical myth narration discussed in this chapter only after I had lived in the Nemiah Valley community for some time. Even then, I encountered it partly by accident. The particular narrative discussed in this chapter was not delivered to me as an individual. It was delivered to me insofar as I was a member of a small group that might appreciate, and in a sense confirm, the personal and cosmological becomings evident in a journey. I encountered this form of narration later than historical narration per se because this form occupies a different place in the community. It serves less as a means for socialization than as a means for, to borrow Bakhtin's phrase, an individual's ideological becoming (1981:342). The conjuncture that it addresses is one that exists within the group and within the self.

Recent commentaries have emphasized that myth narration is more context sensitive or context relevant than past analyses have contended. This material confirms the gist of recent commentaries. Though they seem to enable particular individuals to address matters of transcendent significance, these myth narratives address the particulars of historical experience. In this sense, they are deeply historical.

Like historical narratives, they are used to bridge disjunctures in experience. Historical narratives are used so to bridge the great divide between East and West, between modern and traditional. These are used for the much more delicate task of bridging the divide between the known and the unknown, between the world-present-to-the-senses and the world-evident-in-dreams-and-journeys. In part through the use of intricate patterns of parallelism built up in the narrative text, properties of aesthetic balance and density are imparted to situations and lives that might otherwise be unremarkable. In the process, situations and lives are sanctified and realized.

4. The "New" Discourse of Public Politics

A genre lives in the present, but always remembers its past, its beginning. Genre is a representative of creative memory in the process of literary development. Precisely for this reason genre is capable of guaranteeing the unity and uninterrupted continuity of this development.

M. M. Bakhtin (1984)

Elisa Pine knocked on the door one morning hoping for a ride. Her Nissan pickup truck had inexplicably died on the road in front of our house. Her husband, Len Bouchant, was apparently at home at the east end of the valley. We jumped in my car and drove there. Len Bouchant was about forty-five or fifty years old, of medium height and solid build. He was what some would call a traditionalist. He valued keeping his family self-sufficient by hunting and fishing and exchanging assistance with his family and friends. In the summertime he vacated his reserve house and moved into an outdoor camp beside a lake. He did not interfere with the activities of others, and in return, he chose to go his own way. While the poorest and most traditional looked to him for informal leadership, he generally showed little interest in leading or in the activities of the chief and council. And if the formal leaders thought about him at all, they viewed him with a mix of respect and mild apprehension. Though he would be the first to help if one was stuck or needed a little meat, he could not be counted on to support political agendas.

We arrived at the house, and Elisa invited me in. Len was standing next to a massive masonry chimney and drinking a cup of coffee. He had, as always, a twinkle in his eye. We greeted each other and talked briefly about the weather and then turned to my slow progress in trying to learn the language. He laughed pleasantly at my shortcomings and then turned more serious. He suggested that I study—and as he spoke he pointed to a poster prominently displayed on the wall of his living room—"the declaration." He said that there is a great deal "n it," more than one might think. I nodded, and though I had no idea what he meant, I have remembered what he said to this day. He then finished his coffee, and we all drove back to the stranded pickup truck.

The declaration had been assembled by the formal leadership of the band together with a lawyer as part of an attempt to prevent industrial clear-cut logging from despoiling the traditional territory, a struggle that continues to this day. It was completed a year or so before I arrived, and I had noticed it hanging in almost all the homes in the valley during my stay. Given his apathy toward the activities of the formal leadership, however, I was surprised to see it in Len Bouchant's house. And I was even more surprised that he treated it with respect.

Despite his suggestion I did not study the declaration carefully until some years after completing my fieldwork. One day, far from Chilcotin country and more or less on a whim, I began to examine the Chilcotin portion of the document. Obviously, at one level the document represents an appropriation of the language of nationalism (Anderson 1983, 1992). This is patent in the English portions of the document. When I studied the Chilcotin portions, however, I found that they do not match up with the English. The Chilcotin portions do not represent direct translations. As I continued to translate word by word, I was astonished to discover a direct representation of the voice of the original ancestor of the Chilcotin people. Further analysis of the document and an ethnographic consideration of its place within the community have convinced me that the declaration represents nothing less than one community's attempt to encompass the modern political present within the framework of the traditional culture. Perhaps this is what Len had in mind.

The Study of New Event Genres
In the context of the recent history of expansion of Western market forces and Western political ideas, new "kinds of discursive interaction have been emerging in local communities" (Silverstein 1998:410). The new genres often have a public component, which is to say, they are performed at least in part in the modern public sphere. Ethnographers of speaking have observed that while these new genres are sometimes seen as superseding older ones, they often exhibit real continuities with traditional forms. Michael Silverstein observes that the events in which they are performed present opportunities for emphasizing both continuity and change: "Public events of these kinds particularly become sites not only for social reproduction in the (at least theoretically) homeostatic political organization of a local community; they are increasingly problematic rituals of identity transformation in relation to an expanding field of intersecting cultural allegiances" (1998:411).

For example, forms of discourse produced by native officials in early colonial Maya society "reflect a process of local innovation, blending Maya and Spanish discourse forms into novel types" (Hanks 1987:668). On the one hand, sixteenth-century Mayan elites "sustained the appearance that they held to the same values as their Spanish addressee, that they were themselves legitimate, and that the discourse they created was authoritative" by "invoking dominant ideological and institutional frameworks" (Hanks 1987:688). This was done by fitting the texts into "contemporary Spanish categories such as *carta* (letter), *informacion de derecho* (statement of rights), and *concierto* (agreement)" (Hanks 1987:688). On the other hand, "native conventions also laid claim over official Maya in at least some of its features, and lead to another reading. For instance, the texts are written in Maya, showing indigenous forms of address, along with prose and verse styles common to other kinds of native discourse" (Hanks 1987:688).

The ambivalent quality of these hybrid forms raises questions about how to go about interpreting them. To answer the question of whether they represent continuity or change, for example, requires that we consider whether or not they represent unitary acts. William Hanks, for example, explores how such "texts" "hang together as coherent wholes" (1987:671). Drawing on Mikhail Bakhtin's notion of "finalization," Hanks argues that the completeness of "texts" is established at three levels: locally, at the level of the whole work, and at the global level of the production and reception context (1987:672). Local completeness, he argues, is emphasized by the use of verse constructions, work completeness through metalinguistic specification of genre in the work itself, and completeness of global context through common thematic, stylistic, and constructive features at each of the three levels for all instances of the discourse.

The declaration, on the other hand, seems not to "hang together as a coherent whole." Different people read it in different ways. The declaration only appears to be a single "text" if we consider it as a print artifact without regard for how it is actually "read" by particular parties. What is novel about it is that it seems to facilitate the coexistence of several mutually incompatible readings, some traditional and some modern. Thus, the declaration represents different things for different people. For some it represents the assimilation of a new event genre to a local "traditional" form; for others, the extension of a "traditional" practice; and for yet others, the formation of a ritual of identity transformation (see Silverstein 1998). Based on what we see with the declaration, we might consider the possibility that many new event genres play a role in establishing two things simultaneously: modernity and tradition.

The Circumstances Surrounding the Declaration

From the time British Columbia became a province in 1871, loggers, miners, ranchers, tourists, and native Indians have competed for the use of the Crown (or pubic) lands, which happen to constitute the greatest portion of territory in the province. With the exception of a corner of northwest British Columbia included in a treaty originating in Alberta and several minor allotments near Vancouver, mainland British Columbia was not dealt with in treaties; hence, today there are no reservations. However, Indian rights to the areas they live in have never been explicitly extinguished, and Indian bands are located throughout the province.

Presently most British Columbian Indians, like the Chilcotin, live on "reserves" situated near Crown land. These are small plots of land originally intended as sites from which to administer bands. A few were meant to provide Indians with access to economic resources, but they were kept small, perhaps to ensure that they would not impede the access of others. Reserves tend to be about one to two hundred acres in size, and most bands have two or three. Subsidized housing is built only on the designated reserve land.

Initially, reserve boundaries had little effect on resource availability. Only recently—and in the case of the Nemiah Valley Indian Band, only now—have commercial uses of public lands effectively precluded Native use. The consequent reduction in the resource base is a primary motivation for participating more actively in land management and public politics.

In 1989, with large-scale logging companies and tourism preparing to enter Nemiah Valley, the Nemiah Valley Indian Band issued a declaration that clarifies the outlines of its traditional territory and indicates that it intended to continue to exercise control over the area. The band also gained a legal injunction that has effectively stopped clear-cut logging in the area, at least for the time being. One band member was instrumental in these events. As the logging and tourism industries were making their plans, Ms. Annie Williams was away attending a two-year business college in Chilliwack on the lower mainland. In addition to learning such subjects as accounting and microeconomics, Williams became familiar with the place of public lands in the economy of British Columbia. She became convinced that aboriginal citizens could effectively intervene in the industrial exploitation of public lands. Her first step was to return to Nemiah Valley and run for the office of chief. She ran on what might be considered a realist platform, outlining the nature of the threats to Nemiah Valley and proposing a strategy by which the band could protect itself.

Williams won the election and became Nemiah Valley's first female chief. Quickly she moved to intervene. Her unprecedented strategy was to shift the site of contest away from the immediate locale and place it instead in the public arena of British Columbia. The band's case was difficult to make at the local level because the issue polarized the local population along ethnic lines. Indians formed a minority, and most non-Indians favored logging. Williams realized that the issue took a different shape at the provincial level, where environmentalists and social activists help even the numbers. Moreover, at the provincial level being pro-Indian could be construed as pro-humanitarian rather than antiwhite. Gaining support from non-Indians became a real possibility with the change in the arena of contest.

In order to shift the case to a provincial level, Williams enlisted the assistance of Cindy English, then a graduate student in anthropology at the University of Victoria. English began working with community members to consider how the memories of elders might be documented. She also contacted a prominent Victoria specialist in Indian law to identify the legal advantages of the Nemiah Valley Indian Band's position. In an important 1989 case, the British Columbian courts had ruled that a Musquem man named Ronald Sparrow had the aboriginal right to fish for food in nontreaty areas of the province (Tennant 1990:225). After listening to their concerns, the lawyer decided that the Xeni Gwet'in, the Nemiah Valley Indian Band, could launch a similar case. If the law recognized the right of band members to trap and forage on their traditional territory, it might be possible to argue that the provincial Forest Service had violated that right by permitting logging.

Once the lawyer was involved, the support of the preeminent environmental organization in British Columbia, the Western Canada Wilderness Committee (wcwc), was enlisted. The hope was that the wcwc might help raise money for legal fees. It had been involved in efforts to block clear-cut logging in many other parts of British Columbia and was even working with indigenous peoples to prevent logging in Borneo.

Together, Williams, the band, the lawyer, and the wcwc resolved that they would issue a "declaration" outlining the boundaries and characteristics of what was to be known as the "Nemiah Aboriginal Wilderness Preserve," a designation for the traditional territory of the Chilcotin people of Nemiah Valley, and request an injunction on logging until the question of whether the band had the aboriginal right to trap could be settled in court. The injunction was granted, and the declaration gave the band a measure of recognition in provincial politics.

Reading the Declaration

The declaration was composed by committee, as declarations always are. The evidence from the document itself suggests that the process went something like this: In consultation with the chief and council, the lawyer and the environmentalists wrote up a model "declaration" in English. The date provided in the English portion is 23 August 1989. A committee of Chilcotin Nemiah Valley Band members provided the Chilcotin version. The committee consisted of men and women of roughly thirty to fifty years of age, people literate in English and in Chilcotin, and some elders. The committee composed a text semantically close to the English declaration. The Chilcotin document is dated 1 December 1989. An English version was later published in a book (Glavin and the People of Nemiah Valley 1992).

The declaration is printed on a 2 × 3′ piece of paper made to look like parchment. The English version of the declaration text is printed on the right of the document, and the Chilcotin is on the left. In the center is a portrait of the local mountain and mythological being, Tsil'os.

The layout suggests that the two "texts," the English and Chilcotin, are but parts of a unitary document. The imitation parchment on which both are printed and the figure located in the middle reinforce this. Even certain features of the presentation of linguistic dualities point to some higher unity. For example, the parallel centering and contiguity of the two titles, *Nenduwh Jid Guzit'in* (Thus we want it) and *Declaration*, suggest that they are two ways of representing the same single entity.

The first step in reading the declaration is to ascertain whether the Chilcotin passage is a direct translation of the English. Below, I present the Chilcotin "text" as it appears in the declaration, and then I follow this with a side-by-side presentation of my close translation of the Chilcotin on the left and the original English "text" as it appears in the declaration on the right. Letters on the left allow the reader to see how the lines of the Chilcotin document correspond with the lines of my close translation. The original English has been arranged in parallel with my translation to facilitate comparison, though the two cannot be aligned perfectly because of the differences between the English original and the Chilcotin in the declaration itself.

Chilcotin

a. Nenduwh Jid Guzit'in
b. Nenduwh k'an dzi Gwelu za, ʔinlhi 1989.
c. Nenduwh gadidinh:
d. Xun tsilhqox gwet'in, Xeni deni nidlin,
e. nenduwh jid guzit'in
f. Yedanx xwedeni nen jeʔanajest'in,
g. jedaltsi taʔagunt'ih ʔeyed
h. gwenenazijez ʔeyed
I. nenduwh gadidinh jid guzidzin:
j. Xeni Gwet'in Xa Gwenanisjez
k. Nenduwh Gadidinh,
l. Xeni gwet'in Xagwenanisjez ʔeyed:
m. 1. Lha xedecen bid seniya ʔanats'edulyi gut'in.
n. 2. Lha tsi ts'edulhduz cuh gat'in.
o. 3. Lha ʔeten nats'egutsi gut'in

p.   4. Yes qi nazus gadant'i ?eqats'etat'ilh dza
q.   be?anats'etat'in.
r.   5. Tsilhqox bin, Dasiqox, hink'an Telhiqox
s.   ?eyed lha ts'egulhbanx hink'an nats'u?ilh,
t.   gut'in.
u.   6. Yedanx dzah nenduwh gat'in,
v.   deni nidlin nenk'ed ?eguh gataghat'ilh.
w.   7. Midugh xwenenjiyetayalh nenk'ed se?agunt'ih,
x.   gan xun gweba?anadetaghadilh.
y.   8. Xun xeni gwet'in xwenen gweqa?adidih xuh,
z.   lha ?ilhax xwets'ah tasalh xuh.

Translation of the Chilcotin   **Original English Declaration**

a. Thusly we want it.

b. Here this day of December
   [lit., "ice only"] 1, 1989.

c. We proclaim this: Let it be known as of August 23,
                                     1989

d. we Chilcotin people, being   We, the Tsilhqut'in people of
   people of Nemiah Valley,   Xeni, known as the Nemiah
                                     Valley Indian Band,

e. thus we want it.   declare

f. The land where our people   that the lands shown on the map
   moved about long ago   attached,

g. where they lived well   which form part of our

h. where we live   traditional territory, are, and
                                     shall

i. this is how we want it   henceforth be known as:
   addressed:

j. Nemiah Valley People's   Nemiah Valley Aboriginal
   Territory.   Wilderness Preserve.

k. Thus we proclaim,   Let it be known that:

l. in regard to Nemiah Valley   Within the Nemiah Aboriginal
   People's Territory: Wilderness Preserve:

m. 1. There will be no making money with the use of our timber.

1. There shall be no commercial logging. Only local cutting of trees for our own needs, i.e., firewood, housing, fencing, native uses, etc. . . .

n. 2. There will be no drilling in the mountains [lit., "rock"].

2. There shall be no mining or mining explorations.

o. 3. There will be no road making.

3. There shall be no commercial road building.

p. 4. Motorized snow shoes (snowmobiles)

4. All terrain vehicles and skidoos

q. and off road vehicles can only be used for hunting.

shall only be permitted for trapping purposes.

r. 5. At Chilko Lake, Taseko River, and

5. There shall be no flooding or dam

s. Tatlako Lake no damming or flooding.

construction on Chilko, Taseko, and Tatlyyoko Lakes.

t. there will be.

u. 6. As it was done here long ago,

6. This is the spiritual and economic homeland of our people.

v. that is how people will continue to live now.

We will continue in perpetuity: a) To have and exercise our traditional rights of hunting, fishing, trapping, gathering, and natural resources. b) To carry on our traditional ranching way of life. c) To practice our traditional native medicine, religion, sacred, and spiritual ways.

w. 7. It is alright for non-Indians to use our land,

7. That we are prepared to *share* our Nemiah Aboriginal Wilderness Preserve with non-natives in the following ways:

x. only if we grant them permission.

a) With our permission visitors may come and view and photograph our beautiful land. b) We will issue permits, subject to our conservation rules, for hunting and fishing within our Preserve. c) The respectful use of our Preserve by canoists, hikers, light campers, and other visitors is encouraged, subject to our system of permits.

y. 8. We people of Nemiah Valley, we will fight for our land,

8. We are prepared to enforce and defend our Aboriginal rights in any way we are able.

z. no one will be able to take it.

Comparing the English given in the declaration with my close translation of the Chilcotin, we see that the two titles, *Declaration* and *Nenduwh Jid Guzit'in* (which I have translated closely as 'Thus we want it'), are not semantic equivalents. *Declaration* obviously points to the emergence myth of nationhood, wherein a specific sort of political group is creatively indexed by imagining (by orthographically representing) a natural speech act of the people (see Fliegelman 1993; Looby 1996). Specifically, the reference is to the U.S. Declaration of Independence. *Guzit'in* 'we want it' seems to suggest something else. It is not, for example, the closest semantic equivalent of *declare*; that would be a derivation of *-dih* 'say.' Also, while one can see a certain functional resemblance between the versions of the subheading placed in parallel in the layout, "Let it be known that" and *Nenduwh gadidinh* 'we proclaim' or 'say this,' differences in phrasing again suggest that something in addition to semantic equivalency is motivating the Chilcotin forms. The semantic discrepancies between the two versions are not radical. In facts, it is apparently significant that the two columns represent workable if not unique semantic approximations of one another. Nevertheless, we can see that semantic approximation could be reached in a number of different ways in the document. The specific way it is done suggests that semantic equivalency is not the only motivation for the phrasing of the Chilcotin declaration. If the emergence of nationhood more generally is being indexed in the English, something else is apparently being indexed in the Chilcotin.

Further examination confirms that more readings are available beneath the surface. First, there are at least two readings pertinent to nonnative Canadians: one is pertinent to the practice of law, and the other, to the exercise of public opinion. Second, there are at least two readings pertinent to the Chilcotin community: one is pertinent to the leadership, and one, to rank-and-file Chilcotin people. Each of these readings will be outlined in turn.

Readings Pertinent to the Canadian Public

Perhaps the most straightforward reading is one pertinent to the practice of law. One of the difficulties of Native law is that the activities and aspirations of Native individuals that could be used to establish the integrity of their respective communities in legal terms have rarely been documented. When a lawyer begins work for a poorly documented community such as the Chilcotin, it is important to begin to establish such a record as soon as possible. By indicating that the Nemiah Valley Indian Band recognizes itself as a group with a stake in a specific patch of land as of a specific date, the declaration serves these legal purposes. Both the English and the Chilcotin passages contribute to this end. For the English reader, the dates, band name, and territory are spelled out explicitly. The "1989" appearing in the Chilcotin text, which roughly parallels the English passage concerned with the date, suggests to the English reader that group integrity has subjective reality for the Nemiah people.

The declaration also serves to authorize the interests of the Nemiah Valley Indian Band in the eyes of the non-Chilcotin public by "devoicing" the band's interests. The declaration does not cast the interests of this small group in terms unique to them or of the perspective or emotional character of the particular situation but, rather, in terms of the type of struggle recognized to provide the foundation of modern nation-states and, by analogy, of many indigenous movements. This suggests that to be effective, indigenous declarations need, ironically, to express a subjective, perspectivally grounded opposition to states by publicly invoking the principles of legitimate government ostensibly held by the state.

Presumably, the declaration would be considered infelicitous by the public if the portion in Chilcotin contradicted the portion in English. As can be seen in the translation, the Chilcotin portion is semantically close to the English. Other than a few corresponding items, such as the date, the Chilcotin portion is unintelligible to the non-Chilcotin portion of the public because there is virtually no speaking knowledge of the language outside the community itself and no dictionaries or grammars are available. Nevertheless, as the document is translated the passages are semantically close enough that the two can be reasonably understood as versions of the same "text."

Readings Pertinent to the Chilcotin Community

For the Chilcotin leadership, the declaration is read first as an act in the public sphere. Its significance follows from its recognition by lawyers, environmentalists, and the public at large. Similarly, for rank-and-file members, there is a sense in which the effect of declaring testifies to its validity. But that does not account for the depth of commitment shown for the declaration. Support for the document among rank-and-file band members, despite widespread negative feelings toward environmentalists and lawyers, was and is extensive and deeply felt. During the time of my fieldwork between 1990 and 1992, virtually every family had a copy of the declaration posted on a wall in their homes. Time and time again people would take me over to their copy of the declaration. If I was inquiring about particular words, they would often point out the forms as they are printed on the declaration. I was often told that the document contains a deep message.

Ultimately, the validity of the declaration derives not only from its effectiveness in invoking the public sphere—construed here in the narrow sense as a category, or Durkheimian representation, of bourgeois culture (as in Habermas 1995)—but also from its connections to what is understood as "tradition" within the Chilcotin community. The connections to tradition are made within the community, I submit, by reading the declaration as an abbreviated form of a Chilcotin myth, one not commonly told during my stay but one present in the community nonetheless. The myth is present in the community in different ways for different people. For the elders, it is present in the form of childhood memories of its telling. For literate adults and youth, it is present in the ethnographic record. For the elders, the ethnographic record confirms memories; for the literate, the elder's memories confirm the ethnographic record.

Reference to the myth is established as follows: the Chilcotin phrases that are set in parallel with "Declaration" and "Let it be known that" together reproduce the form and sequence of the culture hero's speech in the central performative act of the Tsilhqut'in myth of ethnogenesis. This is why the "translation" takes its specific form. The form of the translation reproduces the first speech act of the Chilcotin people. By reproducing the first Chilcotin speech act within the declaration, the Chilcotin people project that speech act from what speakers of Standard Average European (SAE) construe as the past onto the unfolding flux that speakers of SAE construe as the present. The declaration establishes an analogy between the first act of the Chilcotin people qua people and their debut in the public sphere. In the remainder of this section I will elaborate on the "myth" in question and illustrate how it is invoked in the declaration.

Working for Franz Boas, the head of the Jesup North Expedition, Livingston Farrand, wrote in 1900 that "incomparably the most elaborate and best known of the Chilcotin tales is that which describes the adventures of the culture hero and transformer, Lendixtcux," represented here as Lhin Desch'osh (being a little dog) (1900:4). Lhin Desch'osh is the name of a dogman. He is the transformer–culture hero responsible for many features of the environment in which the contemporary Chilcotin people live. The plot runs roughly as follows.

A chief and his daughter were living in a village. One night someone came to visit the daughter while she was asleep. She could not determine who it was, but the person returned the next two nights. On the fourth night she resolved to find out who it was and marked him with some white powder. In the morning she discovered that it was not one of the young men of the village but, rather, one of her father's dogs. After a little while she gave birth to three pups. As a consequence, her father gathered the community together and moved away, leaving her, the dog, and the dog-children. She taught the children how to procure food and to clothe themselves. She also managed to transform them into people. With Lhin Desch'osh she was only able to transform him halfway, and so he remained half dog and half human. The family became very successful, and the people who had deserted them returned. The woman's sons and Lhin Desch'osh became unhappy because they were surrounded by so many people, and they resolved to leave. On one occasion they suddenly told her, "We want to move to Chilcotin country." Their mother warned them that in Chilcotin country animal-people killed people. She showed them techniques to prevent the animals from harming them.

The narrative recounts how Lhin Desch'osh and his sons encounter a series of dangerous animal-people. Lhin Desch'osh transforms each into what we now know of as animals. When, however, he transforms the brain it comes out as a frog, which he then throws in the water "because it is so ugly." The actors continue until misfortune befalls them and they transmogrify as features of Chilcotin country.

Several episodes feature Lhin Desch'osh performing the role that Melville Jacobs terms the *announcer* (1959:196, 232). Through speech Lhin Desch'osh transforms dangerous persons into animals, plants, and features of the environment. When he engages an adversary, he or one of his sons "announces" the way that the antagonist will be from that point on. For example, in an encounter with one dangerous person, Lhin Desch'osh proclaims: "Your name will be 'ʔuntses' ['Seagull'], and you will have short legs." The person is thereby transformed into the bird we know as the seagull. The announcement itself represents the transformation of a relationship from one that is wholly consumptive or destructive for the Chilcotin people to one that is more balanced.

The rhetorical expression of the process of transformation and its pertinence to the declaration can be further clarified by reference to a translation of Farrand's version of the Lhin Desch'osh narrative developed collaboratively with the help of several Chilcotin individuals. The translation was made several years prior to my interest in the declaration but has proven to be surprisingly helpful. The announcements in *Lhin Desch'osh* are typically framed by the verb theme *ga-* . . . *-dih* ('say' or 'proclaim this'). As is the case for many of the wordlike entities of Athabaskan languages, this verb theme consists of a dependent prefix (*ga-*) and a stem (*-dih*). Announcements are typically made in direct discourse, that is, they are made in the voice of an actor such as Lhin Desch'osh and are addressed to the subject of transformation.

In the myth narration, tokens of *-dih* are repeatedly used to frame situations in which Chilcotin people confront and then effectively resolve conflicts with other people. Situations facing contemporary Chilcotin people are valorized as "performative" by being treated in the same way as myth events. In myth narration, the use of specific linguistic forms such as *ga-* . . .*dih* is represented to be integral to socially significant actions. In one sense the myth narration shows what language can do, while in another it imparts to certain linguistic forms the capacity for material action. Additionally, by being the prerogative of members of the original Chilcotin family, effective speech is linked to participation in specific kinds of social relationships. The myth documents the power of behaving as a member of a group, provides a model for effective speech, and uses the verb theme *ga-*. . .*-dih* to make the linkage between the two.

A typical transformative episode of the myth goes like this: first, Lhin Desch'osh and the boys travel along their way. Then they encounter one of the animal-persons. Next, the boys recall their mother's warning about such encounters. Finally, Lhin Desch'osh indicates that, the danger notwithstanding, he still "wants/wills" things to be such and such a way. Consider the following instances:

1. *ʔeguh chuh Lhin Desch'osh gadih:*
   'Even then Lhin Desch'osh said this:'
   "bet'an disuyu guzest'in hast'ih," nih.
   ' "I want to smoke its leaves," he said.'

2.   *eguh chuh Lhin Desch'osh gadih:*
     'Even then Lhin Desch'osh said this:'
     "ʔeyi tsa huzest'in."
     ' "I want that beaver." '

Here Lhin Desch'osh indicates that he indeed would prefer things to be other than they are, and he indicates how he would like them to be. Nothing is transformed without Lhin Desch'osh first indicating that he "wants" it to be so.

Thus, pairs of utterances can be identified throughout the myth narrative: the first specifying what is "wanted," and the second, the ways things are to be. The "will/want" transformation pattern is apparent in the relationship between examples 3 and 4 and between 5 and 6:

3.   *Lhin Desch'osh guyi bid ʔets'etesis,*
     'Lhin Desch'osh, that [object] on the gaffing pole,'
     bela sex jilxun ʔeyi,
     'that hook he [Seagull] tied to the end,'
     yelhcud gust'in.
     'he [Lhin Desch'osh] wanted to take it.'

4.   *Lhin Desch'osh gadih:*
     'Lhin Desch'osh proclaimed:'
     "neghuzi ʔeyi ʕuntses' hawet'i,
     ' "your [Seagull's] name will be 'ʔuntses,"'
     "ʔegun nenqits'en ʔinlhes neditsel hawet'i."
     ' "and your legs will be very short." '

5.   *Lhin Desch'osh gagst'a hust'in,*
     'Lhin Desch'osh wanted eagle feathers,'
     bek'a qa.
     'for his arrows.'

6.   *Lhin Desch'osh lha dagisyaz ch'adilil,*
     'To the baby eagles he spared,'
     ʔegun gayelhnih:
     'Lhin Desch'osh proclaimed:'
     "gagulhnaz nent'ox dilhgwelh
     ' "from now on, your nests on top'
     "ch'ed dza, nighun ʔas,
     ' "of hills only, you will make them,'
     "hink'an lha deni ch'adezilhʔis."
     ' "and now you won't kill people." '

The interactional model that obtains between such pairs is also apparent in the position of the Lhin Desch'osh myth as a unit vis-à-vis the realm of daily life. Recall that the journey of Lhin Desch'osh and his sons begins when the people who had initially deserted them return. Lhin Desch'osh and his sons are not happy about this and state their "want" in direct discourse:

> 7. *Xenah ʾilhed gajedih:*
> 'One time they suddenly said:'
> *"Yaw tsilhqut'in nen teghuda,*
> ' "Move to Tsilhqut'in country,'
> *"guzit'in," jedih.*
> ' "we want to," they said.'

This utterance initiates the journey of the first Chilcotin people; all subsequent Chilcotin acts in the myth and all subsequent Chilcotin activities more generally stem from this particular act of "wanting." All subsequent acts are thus in one sense construed as the historical completions of this mythical initiative. The literal significance of the myth is that Lhin Desch'osh and his sons lead the Tsilhqut'in people into Chilcotin country. Their "wanting" initiates the entire process of Chilcotin history.

The myth itself provides no corresponding announcement, or transformation, to the effect that "we are now in and of Chilcotin country." Instead, it seems that it is contemporary Chilcotin people who are expected to realize, or make manifest, a properly Chilcotin country. The events in the myth, including the event of first "wanting," provide the condition for their ability to do so. The deeper significance of the story of Lhin Desch'osh seems to be that a people come into being as such around a place and a purpose.

The title of the declaration, *Nenduwh Jid Guzit'in*, then, reproduces the voice of Lhin Desch'osh and his sons articulating the first "want" of the Chilcotin people. Just as the utterance of "nenduwh jid guzit'in" once opened the era of Chilcotin history, it now opens an era of participation in modern public life. The title of the political act is a replica of the title of the original act of the Chilcotin people. It represents the extension of the ultimate metapragmatic frame from myth time to the contemporary political field. The numbered conditions listed under *gadidinh* 'we say, proclaim' spell out the future in the form of a typical mythical announcement. It can be reinterpreted along the lines of the following: "The people of Nemiah Valley proclaim: (1) there will be no making money with our timber, (2) there will be no drilling in the mountains," and so forth.

As noted above, the declaration is considered authoritative by all elements of the community. In my view it is considered authoritative because it

represents an extension of the myth. Nevertheless, the myth seems to authorize the declaration for leaders and rank-and-file members in very different
ways. For rank-and-file members the authority of the declaration is determined by the opinions of the family heads, the elders. For elders, *guzit'in* 'we
want it' and *gadidinh* 'we proclaim [it to be]' or 'say this' connect the paper
declaration of 1989 to oral accounts presented by their elders. When the
document is read to them, elders recognize the central performative phrases.
The recognition is registered not by explicit reference but in elders' confident acknowledgment of the "truth" of what is said in the document.

Elders' access to writing is mediated by the division of linguistic labor in
the contemporary Chilcotin family; their literate children provide access to
the content of the declaration. The elders' opinions in turn mediate the
readings of rank-and-file community members. The elders serve as linkages
between oral narrative practices and what is on the document. But for the
leaders, the literary "elite" of the community, the reading of the document
is also mediated by the ethnographic authority accruing to the work of
Livingston Farrand and other literary works that are being incorporated
into contemporary life through libraries and public schools. For them, the
declaration represents the ongoing viability of an oral tradition and a literary tradition. It represents the birth of a new discourse of land claims, and it
represents the grounding of present-day discourse in the oldest language of
all, the language of ethnogenesis.

Consequences

The measure of the response and the kind of recognition brought about by
the declaration have become more evident as time and politics have taken
their course. The question of Native land claims became a major issue in the
British Columbia election of October 1991. Natives and many nonnative
urbanites felt that the provincial government had yet to carry out its responsibilities to Native peoples. Native peoples were due compensation for their
displacement from traditional lands. Nonnative nonurbanites, however, felt
that Native peoples deserved no "special treatment." Nevertheless, because
legal ambiguities over questions of aboriginal rights were impeding logging
and mining permits, they too were willing to have the government address
the question of land claims. For them, land claims were a way of restoring
their own access to public resources.

The National Democratic Party (NDP) won the 1991 provincial election in
part because of its stated intention of officially initiating a land claims settlement process. The NDP did not immediately begin settling with bands or
tribes, however, but instead continued negotiating settlements to local im-
passes that had been initiated by the previously incumbent Social Credit

Party. In this way, it reasoned, settlements could be handled according to the exigencies of the area. In the best light, the procedure might be viewed as an attempt to be sensitive to local considerations. In the worst, it might be viewed as a policy of divide and rule.

In the Chilcotin region, where the Nemiah Valley Indian Band had fought for and received injunctions on logging, the government intensified an effort to "mediate" between the interested parties. The interested parties included the Xeni Gwet'in First Nation (as the Nemiah Valley Indian Band came to be known), logging companies, tourism entrepreneurs, representative of a gold-mining venture proposed for the Tazeko Valley (an area clearly within Chilcotin traditional territory), and the Departments of Parks and Recreation, Forestry, and Energy and Mining. After meetings that extended over several years, an agreement was reached. A new provincial park was to be formed out of Crown land. The park would effectively preclude logging on a significant portion of traditional Chilcotin territory. Here I quote the first paragraph of the *Vancouver Sun* story, of 13 January 1994, that broke the news:

> A B.C. government besieged by the largest illegal protest in Cana-
> dian history was to unveil a peace pact today to end another land-
> use war. The same year that police arrested more than 800 people
> at Clayoquot Sound, logging road-blocks near Tofino, a committee
> of cowboys, native Indians, loggers, environmentalists and miners
> peacefully negotiated a regional plan in the Tsilhqut'in west of
> Williams Lake. The centrepiece of the deal they cut is a huge new
> provincial park around Chilko Lake, a park almost as large as
> the entire 260,000 hectare Clayoquot Sound region. For loggers,
> miners, ranchers and other commercial interests that use natural
> resources, the deal means the lifting of a moratorium on resource
> developments in the region outside the new park. An area about
> twice as large as the new park would remain open to resource
> exploitation. And unlike Clayoquot, it's a plan that was negotiated
> by local interest groups, not imposed by politicians or bureaucrats
> in Victoria. (Bohn 1994a:B4)

The new government is portrayed as the harbinger of a new order. As Premier Mike Harcourt's press secretary, Andy Orr, put it, "The government hopes that this will serve as a model for the kind of land-use planning decisions that will take place in other areas of the province" (Bohn 1994a:B4).

The selection of the park name registered the continuing Chilcotin presence in the area. For the Chilcotin people of Nemiah Valley and, whether reluctantly or not, for the government too, the choice indicates a degree of political recognition. On 14 January 1994, Glenn Bohn of the *Vancouver Sun* reported that

> a chunk of the Chilcotin almost as large as the entire Clayoquot sound region has become British Columbia's newest provincial park. Premier Mike Harcourt unveiled a 233,000-hectare park Thursday after his cabinet endorsed a land-use plan negotiated by local loggers, native Indians, ranchers, miners and environmentalists. Instead of arguing at blockades or in the courts, the conflicting interest groups talked for two years, cut a deal and signed a peace pact. At a ceremony in Williams Lake on Thursday, the new park was named Ts'il?os, after a local native Indian legend about a man who argued with his wife and was turned into a mountain. In Williams Lake Harcourt preached the gospel of consensus-based negotiations by local interest groups. "The creation of this park demonstrates how a community can come together and resolve a long-standing land-use conflict," the premier said. (Bohn 1994b:A3)

In an article entitled "Name of Park Derived from Aboriginal Legend," the *Vancouver Sun* further elaborates on the name and its connection to the Xeni Gwet'in:

> B.C.'s newest provincial park is named after an aboriginal legend passed on from generation to generation. It is the legend of Ts'il?os (pronounced Sigh-loss), also known as Mount Tatlow. Here is the story, as related on a plaque presented Thursday to Premier Mike Harcourt by the Nemaiah [sic] Indians:
>
> Long ago, before white settlers moved in, Ts'il?os was once a man. Ts'il?os had a wife named ?Eniyud. They lived in the mountains south of Konni Lake. Even though they had six children together, they had trouble getting along with one another.
>
> One day, Ts'il?os and ?Eniyud got into an argument. ?Eniyud threw her baby on Ts'il?os's lap. She left two children with him and took the other three away. Ts'il?os turned into a rock, along with the three children above Xeni Lake. You can still see the baby on his lap today. ?Eniyud and her three children headed toward Tatlayoko Valley. On her way, she planted wild potatoes. When she arrived on the other side of Tatlayoko Valley, ?Eniyud also turned into a rock. Whenever you find wild potatoes growing, she planted them.

The Elders of Xeni gwet'in say that if you point at Ts'il?os, he will make it rain or snow. He will change the weather, usually when you are on foot or horseback, far from home. ?Eniyud is the same, but meaner. The Elders say when you try to camp around her, she will change the weather. (Vancouver Sun 1994:A3)

The link between name and people was reinforced in the way in which the provincial government chose to represent the park on the ground. The government built a metal plate inscribed with the legend into a stone cairn marking the location of the park. The stone cairn is, however, not situated near the boundary of the park as is conventional or near the eponymous mountain, though the mountain is certainly in clear view. It is situated near the northeastern edge of the traditional territory of the Nemiah Valley Indian Band. Although the location is certainly not intended as formal recognition of Native claims to that land, it perhaps unintentionally or unavoidably registers ambiguity over the status of claims to the land between there and the official park boundary.

The nonnative portion of the public recognized that the selected park name had political implications. These were not addressed as such, however—something that would have been difficult to do in this situation without appearing to be uncharitable to Native peoples. Rather, the political implications were displaced to the plane of linguistic representation. Comments ostensibly about the language and orthography of the park name represented for some a sense that the political arrangement between the state and the Indian band was taking on a new and potentially worrisome direction. For example, on 19 January 1994, in a letter to the editor appearing on the op-ed page of the *Vancouver Sun*, H. Musgrove of Vancouver commented as follows:

The B.C. government should be applauded for the new park surrounding Chilko Lake. If the deal was one that the loggers, native Indians, ranchers, miners and even environmentalists could agree on, it is truly a day to celebrate. Hopefully this process could be used again.

But by what idiotic process—if any—did they choose the name Ts'il?os? It's a nice legend that the name comes from, but the word itself is unpronounceable. Ts'il?os Pronounced Sigh-loss? The last time I checked, English was the language of common verbal communication here.

And before the politically correct thought police arrive to falsely accuse me of anti-aboriginal thinking, let me say that I have

nothing against using aboriginal names for places. Capilano,
Matsqui and Kitsilano are all great names.
But please notice that they do not have punctuation in the
middle of the word where some letters are supposed to be.
So how's about Chilko Provincial Park instead? Or Chilcotin?
Or any name without punctuation in it. (1994:A10)

As is noted above, Chilcotin is a term strongly connected to the nonnative community in the area. Even the phrase "native of the Chilcotin" is sometimes used to designate nonnative residents. Similar practices throughout the province indicate that place-names of aboriginal derivation are acceptable—even desirable—as long as they are not linked to contemporary aboriginal communities. This seems to be what is really at issue in relation to the name Tsil'os. The glottal stop, represented in this book with ʔ or an apostrophe, is often represented with a question mark in practical orthographies, is ubiquitous in the speech of the peoples indigenous to what is now British Columbia, and is completely absent in the orthographic representation of English. The intersection of these facts makes the use of the question mark to represent the glottal stop well suited to signaling, to the readers of the *Vancouver Sun*, a Native people's entry into the public sphere.

Even in the public contestation of their orthography, Chilcotin people of the Nemiah Valley Indian Band were reassured that something new was coming about. The Nemiah Valley Indian Band had moved from unratified periphery to—at least for a moment—ratified front and center, in dialogue with the provincial government and the national pubic about the allocation of resources. The recognition signaled a major development.

Conclusion

In certain respects the declaration might be seen as representative of the new forms of discourse that anthropologists are seeing emerge around the world. These discourses are bilingual, culturally hybrid, and temporally complex; one cannot help but wonder what holds them together as unified wholes. If the declaration is any indication, perhaps we might consider the possibility that these forms are being used to address the contradictions presented by modern life and that they have no single unity. What holds them together varies according to the perspectives from which they are viewed.

The novelty of the Chilcotin declaration is tempered by its connections to the oral narrative tradition. It is connected directly to a pattern of interaction given in the words of the culture hero in the origin myth. The linguistic evidence for the presence of the myth is definitive; the sequence of "wanting" and "pronouncing" and the formal identities of the respective verbs leave no question that the myth serves as the rhetorical template for the Chilcotin portion of the declaration.

Non-Chilcotin people read the document according to their own experiences. For many it evokes the aspirations of a nation by analogy to the U.S. Declaration of Independence. Chilcotin elders who are in many ways skeptical of the new ways of their leaders accept the declaration because they view it as a continuation of a traditional myth. Members of younger generations who may not have experienced this myth in the way that their elders did have encountered it in print in the anthropological record. They too see the possibility that the declaration serves as a continuation of a traditional myth. Their elders confirm this point for them. And both of these generations sense that the placement of the myth in a viable form of public discourse provides for its transmission to future generations.

Conclusion

*Western Apache history as practiced by Apaches advances no theo-
ries, tests no hypotheses, and offers no general models. What it
does instead, and likely has done for centuries, is fashion possible
worlds, give them expressive shape, and present them for contemplation as images of the past that can deepen and enlarge
awareness of the present.*

Keith Basso (1996)

James Harvey Robinson conceived of an approach to history that went
beyond political questions to "embrace social, cultural, and especially economic developments." The New History stands to this day as an impressive
attempt to reconcile intellectual imagination, professional history, and the
real challenges facing the modern world (Ritter 1986:299; Robinson 1912).
The people of Nemiah Valley have a limited interest in professional history,
they have even less interest in intellectual movements, and they certainly
were not free to choose among ideas the way Robinson was. Nevertheless,
Robinson's New History can be used to bridge the distance between the
history of Western academics and the history practiced by members of the
Chilcotin community at Nemiah Valley. Chilcotin history shares with the
old (political) history an interest in the powerful institutions and practices
of the past. It shares with Robinson's New History the belief that the generative institutions of the past were not exclusively political and the idea that
history has real application in the present.

   In the end, though, Chilcotin history differs from all varieties of aca-
demic history, in that, as Keith Basso observes of Apache history, it "advances no theories, tests no hypotheses, and offers no general models. What
it does instead, and likely has done for centuries, is fashion possible worlds,
give them expressive shape, and present them for contemplation as images
of the past that can deepen and enlarge awareness of the present" (1996:32).
Which anthropological approach is suited to this history? A Marxist approach (e.g., Wolf 1982) underscores the role played by the economy (in the
sense of the way people make a living) in shaping people's ideas about the
past. This approach is helpful for understanding the thematic content of
Chilcotin historical narratives. For example, historical narratives per se tend
to represent scenarios that might result in changes to the community's way
of life (as seen in chapter 2). Why the narrative emphasis on economic
change? Marxist approaches suggest that we look to the material conditions
of the present for an answer, and sure enough, government contracts, wage

work, and welfare have made, and are making, real incursions into the traditional hunting and gathering and ranching economies. The emphasis on economic change in thematic content can be understood, then, as part of an attempt to come to terms with very material changes.

Going beyond this sort of loose correlation between way of life and historical content, however, presents problems for a Marxist approach. The basic idea behind Marxism is that economic practices determine beliefs. Understanding a body of beliefs requires identifying *the* determining economic practices. Native Americans typically put together their lives by doing a little bit of this and a little bit of that. Within the span of a couple months individuals help cousins with fencing contracts, work as a teaching assistants, hunt, take temporary welfare, receive dried salmon from siblings, sell cows, substitute at the local post office, and drag neighbor's hunted game out of the woods. Part-time capitalists, part-time peasants, part-time hunter-gatherers—how is one to decide which economic practice determines which belief, or, in other words, how is one to determine which "mode of production" is generative of which ideology?

One approach would be to use economics to decide. But even if it were possible to determine which economic practices make the most economic impact, Chilcotin people choose to weight some activities more than others on other grounds. Moreover, historical narrative practices, what I am trying to explain here, play a part in weighting economic activities relative to one another. In other words, historical narrative practices play a part in determining which economic practices have broader cultural implications. Obviously, it is impossible to give a complete economic explanation of an activity that determines when and how economics counts. In sum, then, a classic Marxist approach is necessary for setting the scene for the study of Chilcotin narrative practices, and is somewhat useful for guiding content analysis, but in and of itself it is inadequate for guiding a more detailed inquiry.

Recent "new Marxist" work that explores the possibility that nationalism originates as a response to dynastic oppression (Anderson 1983, 1992) also seems to have application. This work is helpful, for example, in trying to understand why the people of Nemiah Valley recently issued a declaration. Why would a group of Native Americans, who have been harassed by Westerners for the last 100 years, suddenly take up a quintessentially Western form of political expression? Anderson shows that nationalism and its symbolism cannot be understood in terms of cultural continuities. For starters, he observes that although it has become associated with Europe, nationalism was not a European invention. It first originated in the Americas when colonial creoles united with indigenous peoples in opposition to the dynastic orders of colonial administrations. Academically speaking, in other words, declarations and other nationalistic linguistic gestures are not exogenous to the Americas or to Native Americans. The trappings of nationalism could in fact be used by Native Americans to emphasize the continuity of the tradition. While there is much to be said for this line of thinking, it simply does not apply to the materials examined here.

What is more to the point in the new Marxism is Benedict Anderson's observation that nationalism tends to arise when people sense that their social mobility is obstructed in some larger field of social relations. In other words, Anderson suggests that nationalism is born not of a particular historical or cultural tradition but, rather, of a set of structural circumstances. And this set of structural circumstances happens to be endemic in contemporary Native North America. Thus, his work suggests that the Chilcotin declaration is an intelligible attempt to address political and economic subjection within the political economic order of contemporary Canada.

What is most remarkable about the Chilcotin declaration, nevertheless, is not that leaders used the symbolism of nationalism to address the Canadian public in regard to oppression but that all the band members, from the politically involved to the politically peripheral, acknowledged and continue to acknowledge the declaration's authenticity and authority. The challenge is thus to account for the meanings people attribute to this and related contemporary verbal gestures.

The approach best suited to the study of verbal gestures and communicative practice more generally is the ethnography of speaking (Bauman and Sherzer 1974, 1989; Hymes 1962, 1964). The ethnography of speaking was developed around two focuses, the investigation of the patterning of linguistic styles within the community and the analysis of unfolding events (Hymes 1962). Roman Jakobson's model of essential communicative factors and functions served as the framework of the analysis of unfolding events, and, in slightly modified form, it has proven indispensable in documenting and interpreting specific instances of narration in this study.

No similarly effective model was developed within the ethnography of speaking for guiding the investigation of the patterning of linguistic styles within the community. Such anthropological concepts as were used (e.g., "community") did not receive the same degree of scrutiny as the linguistic conceptual repertoire. In effect, by not explicitly orienting itself to one or another approach to social analysis, the ethnography of speaking depended on a generic functionalism. In practice this meant that linguistic varieties were to be mapped in relation to "communities," conceptualized as unitary segmentable wholes.

While not without a certain heuristic utility, such crude modeling of community is inadequate to the task of exploring the ordering of life in contemporary Native North America, where, as Lévi-Strauss noted long ago (1963), communities seem to be organized in one way from one point of view and in another way from another point of view. For "community" to have any utility as an independent variable, it must have some independent reality. Contemporary Native North American "communities" are fast-moving entities. They have repeatedly accommodated economic and political initiatives that have originated in the larger society around them. They have adopted new institutions to old purposes and old ones to new purposes to the point at which it is essentially impossible for an outsider to say which are the operative local structures. In a real sense the "community" *is* organized one way for one purpose and another way for another purpose according to a logic that is shaped by the very communicative practices that the idea of "community" is supposed to explain. In other words, while the ethnography of speaking emphasizes the role of communicative practice, and for good reason seems better suited to study of narrative history than historical materialism, in the end it is dependent on the very same functionalist approach to social analysis.

The contemporary Native North American situation requires an approach that is open to the possibility that culturally specific communicative practices can be formative of social reality, that communicative practices can play a part in weighting economic and political practices relative to one another. Historical anthropology has been revitalized in debates over the interpretation of events that look one way from one point of view and another way from another. Was the escape of Cheyenne warriors from the American army in the winter of 1874–75 a historical accident or the result of a sacred ritual "after [the performance of] which they were invisible to the white soldiers" (DeMallie 1993:525; cf. White 1998:225)? Did Captain Cook's visit to Hawaii represent the encompassment of Polynesia within modern history, or did it represent the incorporation of a man into Hawaiian cosmology (Sahlins 1985)? Was the American Revolution a "real event for Native Americans or an unmarked interval in a continuing series of struggles that had begun long before 1776 and would continue after the British surrender at Yorktown" (Fogelson 1989:142; cf. Calloway 1995:xiv)? Although many care deeply about these questions, answers have proven elusive. Historical anthropologists have contributed to such debates by attempting to describe the processes through which historical realities are determined. To some extent, all agree, historical realities are constrained by material circumstances and the basic functional requirements of all humankind. Beyond that, however, people interpret unfolding events by reference to cultural traditions of interpreting unfolding events. Understanding what really happened requires making reference to what people thought was really happening. Understanding what people thought was really happening requires making reference to the relevant cultural traditions of historical interpretation. Historical anthropology, with its focus on how people make sense of the multiple realities they confront in the modern world, then, is the missing link between the ethnography of speaking and the social analysis of the contemporary community at Nemiah Valley. Members of the Nemiah Valley Indian Band continue to make sense of the world according to their own traditions of historical interpretation. This is a dynamic tradition to be sure, integral to effective action in this twenty-first century, but it represents importantly a way of making meaningful the expanding connections between the present and the past. And thus in this study each of these approaches has been used to a point. Marxism was used to identify what might be the biggest challenges facing the contemporary community at Nemiah Valley. Historical anthropology, a branch of cultural anthropology, was used to emphasize the extent to which members of the Nemiah Valley Indian Band are defining contemporary reality in accord with a long-standing cultural tradition. And the ethnography of speaking was used to guide the contextualization of unfolding narrative events. It is my hope that the reader will come away from this study with some understanding of how vernacular history is practiced in small communities today, with a sense of the aesthetic richness of such practices, and with an appreciation of the remarkable integrity of contemporary Chilcotin culture.

References

Anderson, Benedict
1983   Imagined Communities: Reflections on the Origins and Spread
        of Nationalism. London: Verso.
1992   Imagined Communities: Reflections on the Origins and Spread
        of Nationalism. Revised edition. London: Verso.

Austin, J. L.
1962   How to Do Things with Words. Cambridge MA: Harvard
        University Press.

Bakhtin, M. M.
1981   The Dialogic Imagination. Austin: University of Texas Press.

Bakhtin, M. M., and P. N. Medvedev
1968   The Formal Method in Literary Scholarship: A Critical
        Introduction to Sociological Poetics. Baltimore: Johns Hopkins
        University Press.

Basso, Keith H.
1979   Portraits of "the Whiteman": Linguistic Play and Cultural
        Symbols among the Western Apache. Cambridge: Cambridge
        University Press.
1996   Wisdom Sits in Places: Language and Landscape among the
        Western Apache. Albuquerque: University of New Mexico
        Press.

Bauman, Richard
1986   Story, Performance, and Event: Contextual Studies of Oral
        Narrative. Cambridge: Cambridge University Press.

Bauman, Richard, and Charles L. Briggs
1990   Poetics and Performance as Critical Perspectives on Language
        and Social Life. Annual Review of Anthropology 19:59–88.

Bauman, Richard, and Joel Sherzer
1974   Explorations in the Ethnography of Speaking. Cambridge:
        Cambridge University Press.
1989   Explorations in the Ethnography of Speaking. 2nd edition.
        Cambridge: Cambridge University Press.

Boas, Franz
1894   Chinook Texts. Bureau of American Ethnology Bulletin, 20.
        Bureau of American Ethnology, Washington DC.

1901   Kathlamet Texts. Bureau of American Ethnology Bulletin, 26. Bureau of American Ethnology, Washington DC.

1902   Tsimshian Texts. Bureau of American Ethnology Bulletin, 27. Bureau of American Ethnology, Washington DC.

1916   Tsimshian Mythology. Based on Texts Recorded by Henry W. Tate. *In* 31st Annual Report of the Bureau of American Ethnology for 1909–1910. Pp. 29-1037. Bureau of American Ethnology, Washington DC.

Boas, Franz, and George Hunt

1912   Tsimshian Texts. Publications of the American Ethnological Society, n.s., III. American Ethnological Society, Leiden.

Bohn, Glenn

1994a   Big Piece of Chilcotin Becomes Newest Park. Vancouver Sun, 13 January: B4.

1994b   Chilcotin Provincial Park Peace Place Aims to Avoid Eruption of Range War. Vancouver Sun, 14 January: A3.

Booth, Wayne

1996   Types of Narration. *In* Narratology: An Introduction. Susana

[1961] Onega and José Angel Barcia Landa, eds. Pp. 145–154. New York: Longman.

Briggs, Charles, and Richard Bauman

1992   Genre, Intertextuality, and Social Power. Journal of Linguistic Anthropology 2(2):131–172.

1999   "The Foundation of All Future Researches": Franz Boas, George Hunt, Native American Texts, and the Construction of Modernity. American Quarterly 51(3):479–528.

Brody, Hugh

1988   Maps and Dreams: Indians and the British Columbia Frontier. Vancouver, British Columbia: Douglas and McIntyre Ltd.

Calloway, Collin G.

1995   The American Revolution in Indian Country: Crisis and Diversity in Native American Communities. Cambridge: Cambridge University Press.

Casagrande, Joseph B.

1959   Some Observations on the Study of Intermediate Societies: Intermediate Societies, Social Mobility and Communication. Seattle: American Ethnological Society.

Cohn, Bernard S., and McKim Marriott
1958   Networks and Centers in the Integration of Indian Civilization.
        Journal of Social Research 1:1–9.

Collins, James
1998   Understanding Tolowa Histories. New York: Routledge.

Cruikshank, Julie
1998   The Social Life of Stories: Narrative and Knowledge in the
        Yukon Territory. Lincoln: University of Nebraska Press.

Dahlstrom, Amy
1992   Plains Cree Morphosyntax. New York: Garland Publishing, Inc.

Darnell, Regna
1974   Correlates of Cree Narrative Performance. *In* Explorations in
        the Ethnography of Speaking. Richard Bauman and Joel
        Sherzer, eds. Pp. 315–336. Cambridge: Cambridge University
        Press.

DeMallie, Raymond J.
1993   "These Have No Ears": Narrative and the Ethnohistorical
        Method. Ethnohistory 40(4):515–538.

Dinwoodie, David W.
1999   Textuality and the "Voices" of Informants: The Case of Edward
        Sapir's 1929 Field School. Anthropological Linguistics
        41(2):165–192.

Duranti, Alessandro
1984   Lauga and Talanoaga: Two Speech Genres in a Samoan
        Political Event. *In* Dangerous Words: Language and Politics in
        the Pacific. Don L. Brenneis and Fred R. Myers, eds. Pp. 217–
        237. New York: New York University Press.

Farrand, Livingston
1900   Traditions of the Chilcotin Indians. Memoirs of the American
        Museum of Natural History 4(1):1–54.

Finnegan, Ruth
1970   Oral Literature in Africa. Nairobi: Oxford University Press.

Fliegelman, Jay
1993   Declaring Independence: Jefferson, Natural Language, and the
        Culture of Performance. Stanford: Stanford University Press.

Fogelson, Raymond D.
1989   The Ethnohistory of Events and Nonevents. Ethnohistory
        36(2):133-147.

French, David
1958   Cultural Matrices of Chinookan Non-Casual Language.
        International Journal of American Linguistics 24:258–263.

Gennette, Gerard
1980   Narrative Discourse. Ithaca: Cornell University Press.

Glavin, Terry, and the People of Nemiah Valley
1992   Nemiah: The Unconquered Country. Vancouver, British
        Columbia: New Star Press.

Goffman, Erving
1974   Frame Analysis: An Essay on the Organization of Experience.
        New York: Harper and Row Publishers.
1981   Forms of Talk. Philadelphia: University of Pennsylvania Press.

Goldman, Irving
1940   The Alkatcho Carrier of British Columbia. In Acculturation in
        Seven American Indian Tribes. Ralph Linton, ed. Pp. 333–389.
        New York: Appleton-Century.

Gossen, Gary
1974   Chamulas in the World of the Sun. Cambridge: Cambridge
        University Press.

Gumperz, John J.
1964   Speech Variation and the Study of Indian Civilization. In
        Language in Culture and Society. Dell Hymes, ed. Pp. 416–428.
        New York: Harper and Row Publishers.
1968   Types of Linguistic Communities. In Readings in the Sociology
        of Language. Joshua A. Fishman, ed. Pp. 460–472. The Hague:
        Mouton.

Habermas, Jürgen
1995   The Structural Transformation of the Public Sphere: An
[1962] Inquiry into a Category of Bourgeois Society. Thomas Burger
        with Frederick Lawrence, trans. Cambridge MA: MIT Press.

Halbwachs, Maurice
1992   On Collective Memory. Lewis A. Coser, trans. Chicago:
[1941] University of Chicago Press.

Hanks, William F.
 1986   Authenticity and Ambivalence in the Text: A Colonial Maya
        Case. American Ethnologist 13(4):721–744.
 1987   Discourse Genres in a Theory of Practice. American
        Ethnologist 14(4):668–692.

Hill, Jane H.
 1985   The Grammar of Consciousness and the Consciousness of
        Grammar. American Ethnologist 12:725–737.
 1986   The Refiguration of the Anthropology of Language. Cultural
        Anthropology 1:89–102.
 1995   The Voices of Don Gabriel: Responsibility and Self in a
        Modern Mexicano Narrative. In The Dialogic Emergence of
        Culture. Dennis Tedlock and Bruce Mannheim, eds. Pp. 97–
        147. Urbana: University of Illinois Press.

Hymes, Dell
 1962   The Ethnography of Speaking. In Anthropology and Human
        Behavior. Pp. 13–53. Washington DC: Anthropological Society
        of Washington.
 1964   Introduction: Toward Ethnographies of Communication.
        American Anthropologist 66(6), pt. 2:12–25.
 1981   "In Vain I Tried to Tell You": Essays in Native American
        Ethnopoetics. Philadelphia: University of Pennsylvania Press.

Jacobs, Melville
 1959   The Content and Style of an Oral Literature: Clackamas
        Chinook Myths and Tales. Viking Fund Publications in
        Anthropology, 26. New York: Viking Fund.
 1968   An Historical Event Text from a Galice Athabaskan in
        Southwestern Oregon. International Journal of American
        Linguistics 34(3):183–191.

Jakobson, Roman
 1971   Selected Writings. The Hague: Mouton.

Lane, Robert Brockstedt
 1953   Cultural Relations of the Chilcotin Indians of West Central
        British Columbia. Ph.D. dissertation, University of
        Washington.

Lévi-Strauss, Claude
 1963   Structural Anthropology. New York: Basic Books.

1968   The Story of Asdiwal. *In* The Structural Study of Myth and Totemism. Edmund Leach, ed. Pp. 1–47. London: Tavistock Publications.

Looby, Christopher
1996   Language, Literary Form, and the Origins of the United States. Chicago: University of Chicago Press.

McLaughlin, Daniel
1992   When Literacy Empowers: Navajo Language in Print. Albuquerque: University of New Mexico Press.

Moore, Robert E.
1993   Performance Form and the Voices of Characters in Five Versions of the Coyote Cycle. *In* Reflexive Language: Reported Speech and Metapragmatics. John A. Lucy, ed. Pp. 213–240. Cambridge: Cambridge University Press.
In press   Language in Cultural Diorama. Cultural Anthropology.

Munn, Nancy D.
1992   The Cultural Anthropology of Time: A Critical Essay. Annual Review of Anthropology 21:93–123.

Musgrove, H.
1994   What Kind of Name Is This for B.C.'s Newest Park? Letter to the Editor, Vancouver Sun, 19 January: A10.

Onega, Susana, and José Angel Garcia Landa
1996   Narratology: An Introduction. London: Longman.

Parks, Douglas, and Raymond J. DeMallie
1992   Plains Indian Literatures. boundary 2:19(3):105–147.

Parmentier, Richard J.
1993   The Political Function of Reported Speech. *In* Reflexive Language. John Lucy, ed. Pp. 261–286. Cambridge: Cambridge University Press.

Ritter, Harry
1986   Dictionary of Concepts in History. New York: Greenwood Press.

Robinson, James Harvey
1912   The New History: Essays Illustrating the Modern Historical Outlook. New York.

Sahlins, Marshall
1985   Islands of History. Chicago: University of Chicago Press.

Sapir, Edward
1909   Wishram Texts; Together with Wasco Tales and Myths. Jeremiah Curtin, collector; Edward Sapir, ed. Publications of the American Ethnological Society, 2. American Ethnological Society, Leiden.

Scott, James
1990   Domination and the Arts of Resistance: Hidden Transcripts. New Haven: Yale University Press.

Service, Elman
1966   Cultural Evolutionism: Theory in Practice. New York: Holt, Rinehart and Winston, Inc.

Sherzer, Joel
1983   Kuna Ways of Speaking: An Ethnographic Perspective. Austin: University of Texas Press.

Silverstein, Michael
1976   Hierarchy of Features and Ergativity. *In* Grammatical Categories in Australian Languages. R. M. W. Dixon, ed. Pp. 112–171. Canberra: Australian Institute of Aboriginal Studies.
1979   Language Structure and Linguistic Ideology. The Elements: A Parasession on Linguistic Units and Levels, April 20–21, 1979. Paul R. Clyne, W. Hanks, and C. Hofbauer, eds. Pp. 193–247. Chicago: Chicago Linguistic Society.
1985   Culture of Language in Chinookan Narrative Texts; or, On Saying That . . . in Chinook. *In* Grammar Inside and Outside the Clause: Some Approaches to Theory from the Field. Johanna Nichols and Anthony C. Woodbury, eds. Pp. 132–171. Cambridge: Cambridge University Press.
1996a   The Secret Life of Texts. *In* Natural Histories of Discourse. Michael Silverstein and Greg Urban, eds. Pp. 81–105. Chicago: University of Chicago Press.
1996b   Encountering Languages and the Languages of Encounter in North American Ethnohistory. Journal of Linguistic Anthropology 6:126–144.
1998   Contemporary Transformations of Local Linguistic Communities. Annual Review of Anthropology 27:401–425.

1999   Linguistic NIMBYism and Other Voicings from the Culture of Local Languages. Unpublished MS.

Silverstein, Michael, and Greg Urban
1996   Natural Histories of Discourse. Chicago: University of Chicago Press.

Tambiah, Stanley
1985   Culture, Thought, and Social Action: An Anthropological Perspective. Cambridge MA: Harvard University Press.

Tennant, Paul
1990   Aboriginal Peoples and Politics. Vancouver: University of British Columbia Press.

Tyhurst, Robert J. S.
An Ethnographic History of the Chilcotin. Ph.D. dissertation manuscript, University of British Columbia.

Urban, Greg
1984   Speech about Speech in Speech about Action. Journal of American Folklore 97(385):310–328.

Vancouver Sun
1994   Name of Park Derived from Aboriginal Legend. Vancouver Sun, 14 January: A3.

White, Richard
1998   Using the Past: History and Native American Studies. *In* Studying Native America: Problems and Prospects. Russell Thornton, ed. Pp. 217–243. Madison: University of Wisconsin Press.

Whitehead, Margaret
1981   The Caribou Mission: A History of the Oblates. Victoria, British Columbia: Sono Nis Press.

Wilmeth, Roscoe
1978   Anahim Lake Archaeology and the Early Historic Chilcotin Indians. National Museum of Man, Mercury Series Archaeological Survey Paper, 82. National Museum of Man, Ottawa.

Wolf, Eric R.
1982   Europe and the People without History. Berkeley: University of California Press.

Index

IN STUDIES IN THE ANTHROPOLOGY
OF NORTH AMERICAN INDIANS

The Four Hills of Life: Northern Arapaho Knowledge and Life Movement
By Jeffrey D. Anderson

The Semantics of Time: Aspectual Categorization in Koyukon Athabaskan
By Melissa Axelrod

Lushootseed Texts: An Introduction to Puget Salish Narrative Aesthetics
Edited by Crisca Bierwert

People of the Dalles: The Indians of Wascopam Mission
By Robert Boyd

The Lakota Ritual of the Sweat Lodge: History and Contemporary Practice
By Raymond A. Bucko

*From the Sands to the Mountain: Change and Persistence
in a Southern Paiute Community*
By Pamela A. Bunte and Robert J. Franklin

A Grammar of Comanche
By Jean Ormsbee Charney

Reserve Memories: The Power of the Past in a Chilcotin Community
By David W. Dinwoodie

Northern Haida Songs
By John Enrico and Wendy Bross Stuart

Powhatan's World and Colonial Virginia: A Conflict of Cultures
By Frederic W. Gleach

The Heiltsuks: Dialogues of Culture and History on the Northwest Coast
By Michael E. Harkin

Prophecy and Power among the Dogrib Indians
By June Helm

Corbett Mack: The Life of a Northern Paiute
As told by Michael Hittman

The Canadian Sioux
By James H. Howard

The Comanches: A History, 1706–1875
By Thomas W. Kavanagh